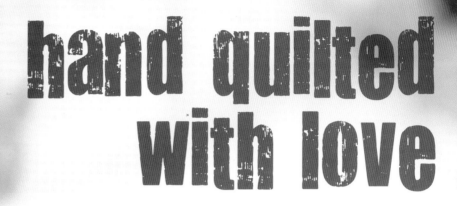

hand quilted
with love

patchwork projects
inspired by a passion
for quilting

Sarah Fielke

CICO BOOKS
LONDON NEW YORK
www.cicobooks.com

Dedication

This book is for my Dad, who is not a quilter.
He is my shelter in a storm.

Published in 2013 by CICO Books
An imprint of Ryland Peters & Small Ltd
20–21 Jockey's Fields   519 Broadway, 5th Floor
London WC1R 4BW   New York, NY 10012

www.cicobooks.com

10 9 8 7 6 5 4 3 2 1

A CIP catalog record for this book is available from the Library of Congress
and the British Library.

ISBN: 978 1 908862 59 4

Printed in China

Editor: Sarah Hoggett
Proofreader: Marie Clayton
Designer: Louise Leffler
Photographer: Sue Stubbs
Illustrator: Stephen Dew

For digital editions, visit www.cicobooks.com/apps.php

contents

introduction

When I started writing this book, it was a jumping-off place. Previous books I have written have had themes—this book, though, is a collection of quilts I've been wanting to make for ages.

What a luxury! I've so enjoyed stretching out creatively, making things because they interested and inspired me, and not because they fit a mold.

With that in mind, I have tried to include a wide spread of quilts, from very easy to quite advanced. There is something for everyone here. The easy quilts will be great for a beginner, or for a more experienced quilter wanting to show off some of their treasured pieces or make a quick gift. The more difficult quilts will, I hope, challenge beginner quilters to stretch out and try something new—and also keep the more experienced quilters interested!

I love making quilts. Making quilts makes me who I am. It's not just the physical stitching of the fabric, although that makes me happy and content. The planning and the sketching and the playing with fabric excites and energizes me, and seeing pattern and color and sparks of ideas in the world around me makes me interested and engaged. Quilting is not just a hobby. Whether you create one quilt a year or upwards of 30 like me, making a quilt is traveling a creative road.

I love making quilts because each one is a puzzle. Finding the right combination of block, scale, color, and surprise is what makes a quilt jump off the page, wall, or bed, and sock you in the heart.

One more thing. Try new things, be adventurous, and crack your own quilting code. Don't be hung up on whether something is right or wrong, or on whether you are a "modern quilter", a "traditional quilter", or even an "art quilter": just be a QUILTER, be creative and love what you do. It's what I do every day—and I can tell you, I'm a happy girl because of it.

choosing fabrics

How many times have I heard the same refrain from my students: "This is the worst part. Can't you just choose my fabrics? I'm so bad with color!" Every time, I'm amazed. The worst part?? Choosing the fabric is the BEST part, as far as I'm concerned. That's the bit where you get to pet the pretty stuff, move it all around, and drool over the designs and beautiful colors. That's where the journey starts—and you should be full of excitement and promise, not dread and confusion!

Most of my quilts contain a lot of different fabrics. I don't usually use one or two greens when I can use 30. While some people think this is incredibly confusing, I actually think this gives me a few advantages.

First, it stops any one fabric from dominating the quilt or unbalancing the other colors. A lot of different greens or blues will create a moving, shifting green or blue tone rather than a solid block of one shade. The different patterns, tones, and scales in all the different fabrics create interest that one fabric on its own simply doesn't have.

Second, I don't ever get stuck finding that PERFECT fabric. Because I'm not looking for one thing, I can't get hung up on what it might be. When I buy fabrics I buy small amounts of lots of different things, unless I really fall in love with something. So when I need 2 meters of red, I can go to my stash and pick out 15 reds, and cut my 2 meters worth from all the different prints I lay my hands to. That way I don't ever have to search every shop for the perfect red or green—I just make my own!

Which leads me to the million-dollar question: how much fabric do I buy?

Well, without giving too much away to the husband (ahem), my general rule is this. If I'm buying a fabric for its usability—because it's a good red or green, or it will go in the "blue stash," or it looks useful—I buy 25 cm. I don't usually buy fat quarters or precuts if I can help it: they're great for a particular project, but being already cut to size, I find them too limiting to stash.

If I like the design and think I might make a bit of a feature of it, I buy half a meter.

Spots on white backgrounds, checks, things that might make a good appliqué background, I always buy one to two meters. Stripes that look good for bindings, never less than 75 cm. Large, blowsy, gorgeous florals that I fall in love with for borders, 2 meters.

And if I really love something and I'm mad for it? I have been known to buy the bolt…

I infamously said in my last book that I don't use solid (plain) fabrics, and quilters have been holding me to it ever since! And so in this book I have made a point of using them, just to show I can! I've tried to use them in the way I would use printed fabrics, though, by mixing them up and putting them with prints and textured fabrics. Paint By Numbers (page 70) was a challenge indeed: I used solids AND jelly rolls, right out of my comfort zone, but I mixed it up with a whole stack of black-and-white prints with a dash of yellow to give me that hop-skip-jump I know so well.

the quilter's workspace

It's not always easy to achieve, and it's certainly not easy to keep tidy—but every quilter needs a workspace. Whether it's something you can put away when you've finished sewing or something more permanent, make sure you have a space to sew that allows you to set up your sewing machine and cutting mat, and hang a design wall.

After your machine (which should have a name, by the way—my sewing machine's name is Bertha), a design wall is your best friend. Being able to lay your blocks out flat in front of you to balance color and perspective—and save your back from crawling on the floor—will change the way you quilt. It also makes it so much easier when you're sewing a difficult design to be able to take something from the wall in order, sew it up, and return it to the wall to see where to sew next.

To make a design wall, you don't have to have a permanent wall, although that does help! If you're lucky enough to have your own sewing studio, you can cover a whole wall of your room with flat polyester batting (not the puffy kind—the kind that looks like a cotton batting) and baste (tack) or pin it in place. Blocks will stick to the batting without pins.

If you need a more portable design wall, try using a large piece of the same batting, or a flannelette sheet, and sewing a pocket into the top to hang over your curtain rods or onto a picture rail. If that fails, pin the sheet to your blinds or your curtains!

And if you REALLY have a small space and have nowhere for any of these, even a largish piece of foam core board from an office supply store covered in flannel will be helpful for laying one or two of your blocks out and looking at them from a distance. Something like this can be stored behind the TV or under your bed.

Once you have your design wall ready for use, you can use it for planning your quilts. I recommend doing this for every quilt in this book, and every other quilt you make, too! Lay out all the pieces for the quilt and move them around until you are happy with the placement of colors. The best way to decide on this is to put all of the pieces on the wall, then look at them through a door peephole (available from a hardware store), a camera lens, or by squinting your eyes. This helps you to see where the dark and light colors fall, so you can balance them out and the quilt looks evenly distributed.

Other essential things in your quilter's workspace are good light and a comfortable chair. Invest in a good lamp for your work area if you don't have natural light, and make sure the chair you sit in is comfortable, and at a good height for your sewing machine so that you don't have to lean over or stretch up to sew.

tools and equipment

General sewing and patchwork supplies

Rather than repeating this list for each project, I am going to assume that you will have the basic requirements before you begin. These include:

* Sewing machine in good working order (unless you are a dedicated hand sewer!) and replacement needles; did you know you should change your machine needle for every new project you start?

* ¼-in. (6-mm) machine foot to fit your machine. Do consider investing in one of these—they are a little pricey but will make a HUGE difference to your stitching and make accurate seams so much easier

* Dressmaking scissors for cutting fabric only

* Scissors for cutting paper or plastic

* Thread snips or small sharp scissors

* Seam ripper

* Straight pins

* Tape measure

* Perspex quilter's ruler—it is handy to have two rulers of the same size to assist in cutting strips without having to turn the cutting mat around

* Rotary cutter (the best one you can afford) and replacement blades

* Self-healing cutting mat

* Masking tape, for securing backing fabric to a flat surface and for marking hand quilting lines without a pencil

* Chalk pencil and gel pen, for marking curved quilting and appliqué lines

* Quilter's safety pins (if you are pinning quilt layers rather than basting; see page 135)

* Quilter's hoop, for hand quilting (this is NOT an embroidery hoop)

* Quilter's thimble

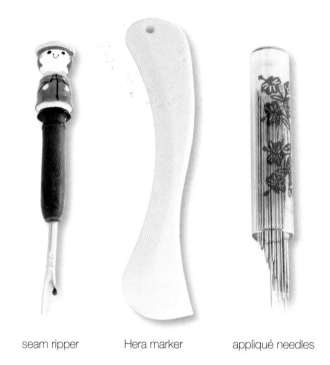

seam ripper   Hera marker   appliqué needles

Mylar circle sets

pincushion

tape measure

thimble

gel pen

tweezer scissors

chalk roller marker

needle case

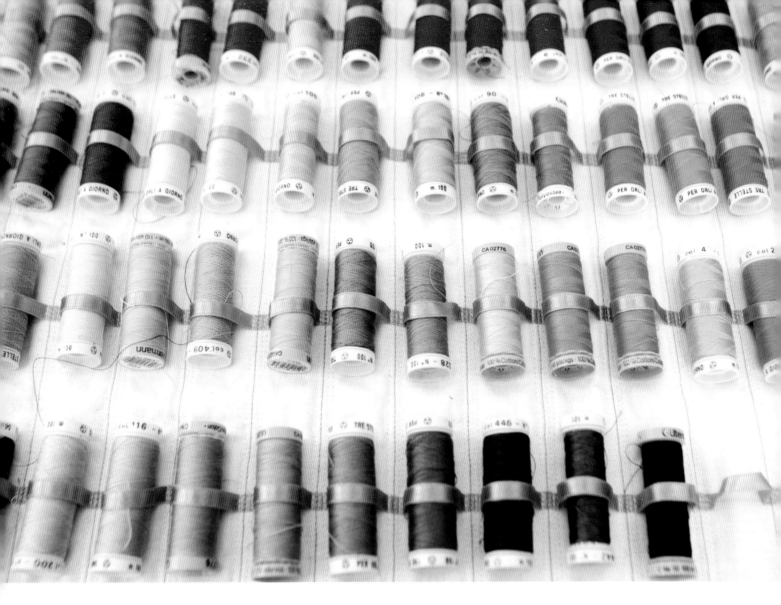

Threads

Match the thread to the fabric when piecing: for example, when using cotton fabric, use cotton thread. Avoid using polyester thread for patchwork—over time, the threads will wear differently and the polyester thread will cut through the fibers of the cotton.

Always use a fine, good-quality thread for your sewing machine. Your machine will produce less fluff sewing with a good-quality material, and your seams will lay flatter and last longer.

In most situations, cream, white, or gray threads are appropriate for piecing—there is no need to change colors to match the fabrics you are sewing. If you are using a multi-colored fabric, use a neutral-colored thread such as beige or gray, and it will blend into the background.

For hand quilting, I use Perle 8 cotton rather than traditional quilting thread. I do this because I like my stitches to stand out and make a statement. Perle cotton is much easier for beginners to handle—you can take larger stitches (up to ¼ in./6 mm in length), and you use a longer, thicker needle than for traditional quilting. For more information on quilting, see pages 136–138.

Specialty rulers

All the quilts in this book can be made using a standard 24-in. (60-cm) quilter's ruler and the templates provided. Occasionally, however, I have included a specialty ruler in the Material Requirements lists. These rulers make cutting much quicker and easier and, if you wish to use them, by all means do so. They are usually sold with detailed instructions for their use.

Half-square triangle ruler

A half-square ruler, also called a 45-degree triangle ruler, is useful but not strictly necessary for cutting half-square triangles. You can, of course, cut these triangles using a standard quilter's ruler by cross cutting strips into squares, then cross-cutting each square in half on one diagonal, giving two half-square triangles. (The size of the square that you cut when cutting half square triangles in this way should always be ⅞ in. (2.25 cm) larger than the desired finished size of the triangle.)

Specialized half-square triangle rulers, however, have already allowed for the seam allowance at the point of the triangle, thus eliminating the "ears" on the seam. This means that if you are using a half-square triangle ruler, you will cut the triangles from a strip of fabric rather than squares, and the size of your strip should be only ½ in. (12 mm) larger than the desired finished size of the triangle, not ⅞ in. (2.25 cm). The half-square triangles you cut with this ruler will have a blunt point for easy alignment and will require less trimming.

A half-square triangle ruler can be used to cut the triangles in Paint By Numbers, Made To Measure, All That And The Hatter, Lady Marmalade, Made In Cherry, and Ups And Downs.

Wedge ruler

Wedge rulers, also called circle segment, fan, or Dresden plate rulers, are used for cutting accurate segments of a circle—or wedges—and come in a variety of brands, sizes, and angles. In this book I used an 18-degree wedge ruler to cut the wedges in Fancy That (page 96).

60-degree triangle ruler

This ruler is used primarily to cut equilateral triangles (each internal angle is 60 degrees and all three sides are the same length), but it is also useful for accurately cutting diamonds, half-diamonds, and 30-degree triangles. I used this ruler for Love Beads (see page 42).

Perspex ruler sets are available for several of the quilts in this book; please see page 156 for details.

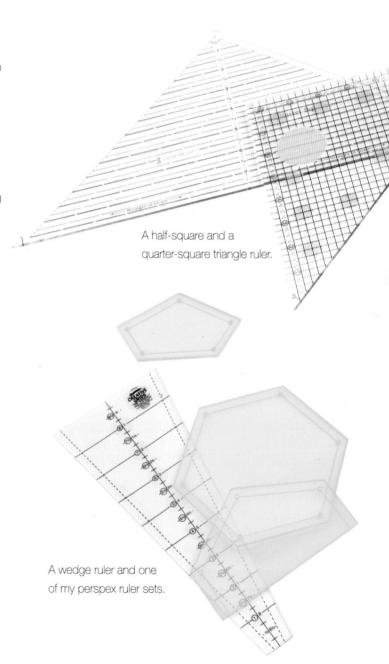

A half-square and a quarter-square triangle ruler.

A wedge ruler and one of my perspex ruler sets.

the projects

Each of the projects takes you step by step through the construction of the quilt top. When you're ready to combine your completed top with the batting (wadding), backing and binding, turn to the Techniques section on page 126 for detailed instructions.

Before you start your project, make sure that you have ironed your fabric flat so you cut accurately. I don't wash my fabric because it takes off the sizing and makes the fabric more difficult to cut; this is a personal preference, however—so if you want to wash, wash! There is no need to wash for color fastness, though. These days, dyes are very good and if you have bought a good-quality patchwork-weight fabric and not a cheapie, the dye shouldn't run. If you are worried about a very dark blue or a red, simply boil the kettle, put a little corner of the fabric in a white cup or bowl, and pour the boiling water over it. If no color comes out, then the fabric is just fine; if it does, then perhaps wash it with a color catcher or some salt in the washing machine.

For all the projects in this book, I recommend that all fabric be 100 percent cotton or linen. I don't like to use poly blends in my quilts, but that's also up to you! Unless otherwise stated, all seams are ¼ in. (6 mm) throughout, and all strips are cut across the width of the fabric, from fold to selvage (selvedge).

This almost goes without saying—but make sure you read the pattern carefully before you start! Many a good project has been spoiled halfway through by the discovery of a step you weren't expecting. Better to be safe than sorry.

The Quilts

I've arranged the quilts in order of difficulty, grading them as follows:

✿ Quick, easy, straight lines, and half-square triangles. Suitable for beginners or experienced quilters who want a fun, friendly project.

✿✿ Slightly more complex, requires techniques such as strip piecing, hand appliqué, piecing diamonds.

✿✿✿ Quilts that require more than one technique, complex color placement, or more advanced piecing. Includes Y seams, crazy piecing, deconstructed piecing, and hand appliqué.

✿✿✿✿ These quilts require several techniques and more complex piecing and color decisions for experienced quilters. If you're not sure, have a go! You never know until you try.

rosewater

This is such a light and pretty throw! Mix large- and medium-size print fabrics so that you create contrasts of scale: if all the print patterns were similar in size, the effect would be overpowering, as there would be nowhere for the eye to rest.

Instructions are given for you to make this quickie in several sizes—use some of your favorite bold patterns and try some creative colorways of your own. You may surprised at how different it can look: my original version of this quilt was in a graphic black-and-charcoal colorway, which has a much bolder, more contemporary feel—see page 22.

Finished size:

Throw, 70½ in. (179 cm) square

Material requirements:

20 in. (50 cm) each of 9 light pink and white fabrics

20 in. (50 cm) green-and-white striped fabric for sashing

22 in. (55 cm) multi-colored striped fabric for binding

4½ yd (4 m) floral fabric for backing

2¼-yd (2-m) square piece cotton batting (wadding)

Cotton thread for piecing

Rotary cutter, mat, and ruler

Sewing machine

General sewing supplies

Cutting:

From each of the pink and white fabrics, cut:

• Three strips, 6½ in. (16.5 cm) wide. Cross cut a piece measuring 6½ x 5½ in. (16.5 x 14 cm) from one end of two of the strips in each fabric and then cut all the remaining strips into pieces measuring 6½ x 10½ in. (16.5 x 26.75 cm).

From the green-and-white striped sashing fabric, cut:

• 15 strips, 1½ in. (4 cm) wide.

From the multi-colored striped binding fabric, cut:

• Seven strips, 3 in. (7.5 cm) wide.

Fabric choices

It is important in this quilt to have a good mix of pattern values. In *Rosewater*, I have used several different large and medium-sized florals, with larger spots and other graphics to create interest and keep the eye moving around the quilt. For *Suit Up* on page 22, even though the colors are very similar and there are no patterns in the suiting fabrics, the pieces of high-contrast feedsack hold the viewer's interest and make the quilt sparkle.

Sewing

1 Lay all the pieces out and move them around until you are happy with the color and pattern placement. In the first and all odd-numbered rows, there are seven 10½-in. (26.75-cm) pieces of fabric; in the second and all even-numbered rows, there are six 10½-in. (26.75-cm) pieces with a 5½-in. (14-cm) piece at each end (see Diagram 1). There are ten rows in total.

2 Sew all the strips together row by row, making sure you keep track of the row numbers. Press.

3 Sew all the rows together, making sure to keep track of the row numbers. Trim ¼ in. (6 mm) from each end of each of the rows with full blocks (that is, rows 1, 3, 5, 7, and 9) to make them 70½ in. (179 cm).

Assembling the quilt top

4 Remove the selvages (selvedges) from the sashing strips. Sew all fifteen 1½-in. (4-cm) strips for the sashing together into one long strip. Press the seams to one side.

5 From this long strip, cut nine pieces each measuring 70½ in. (179 cm). Making the sashing like this ensures that all the joins don't fall in the same place, which allows the eye to pretend they aren't there.

6 Beginning with Row 1, find the center of the row of blocks and the center of a sashing strip. Pin the sashing strip to the bottom of Row 1, right sides together. Pin the ends, then pin in between, easing as you go if needed. Sew the rows together.

7 Repeat this process to join all the rows together and press the seams toward the sashing strips. Your quilt top is complete.

Backing, quilting, and binding

8 Cut the backing fabric crosswise into two pieces, each 81 in. (200 cm) long. Remove the selvages (selvedges) and stitch the pieces together along one long edge. Press the seam allowance open and press the backing piece carefully.

9 If hand quilting, tape the backing fabric right side down to the floor or a very large table using masking tape, smoothing out any creases as you go. Lay the batting (wadding) on the backing fabric, with the quilt top on top. Smooth any creases and hand baste the three layers together, using large stitches and working from the center out. The backing and batting (wadding) should be larger than the top for ease of quilting; don't be tempted to trim them back.

10 Quilt as desired and bind the quilt, following the instructions on pages 136–139.

Want to make this in a different size?

Twin (single) quilt
60½ x 83½ in. (153 x 212 cm)

12 rows down (six full rows and six with a half block at each end), 6 blocks in a full row, 11 sashing rows

Queen-size quilt
97½ x 96½ in. (247.5 x 245 cm)

14 rows down (seven full rows and seven rows with a half block at each end), 9 blocks in a full row, 13 sashing rows

King-size quilt
100½ x 104½ in. (255 x 265.5 cm)

15 rows down (eight full rows and eight rows with a half block at each end), 10 blocks in a full row, 14 sashing rows

Diagram 1

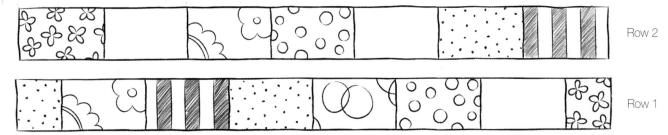

Row 2

Row 1

Note on quilting

Rosewater is machine quilted in a forget-me-not
pattern, using white cotton thread.

variation: suit up

The first quilt that I made using this pattern was this black-and-charcoal version, which was designed as a wedding gift for a couple with a very modern house. The fabrics that I used were all woolen suiting off-cuts, with pieces of old feedsacks mixed in. I love the way such a simple pattern and old, recycled fabrics can make such a bold, modern statement.

made in cherry

This quilt is called *Made In Cherry* because it's made in the Cherry colorway of one of my fabric ranges, *St Ives*. All the colorways are named after my favorite flavors of slushies when I was a kid—Cherry, Watermelon, Polar Purple Shiver, and Blue Vanilla. Remember how they used to change the color of your tongue? Cherry was always my favorite, though, because it made your lips red!

Finished size:

Double quilt, 80½ in. (2 m) square

Material requirements:

20 in. (50 cm) each of eight different red-and-white print fabrics

2½ yd (2.3 m) plain red linen for background

28 in. (70 cm) pink-and-yellow striped fabric for binding

5 yd (4.6 m) backing fabric

2½-yd (2.3-m) square piece cotton batting (wadding)

Cotton thread for piecing

Rotary cutter, mat, and ruler

Sewing machine

General sewing supplies

Cutting:

From each of the red-and-white fabrics, cut:

• Three strips, 4½ in. (11.5 cm) wide. Cross cut these strips into 4½-in. (11.5-cm) squares.

• One strip, 4⅞ in. (12.5 cm) wide. From this strip, cut four 4⅞-in. (12.5-cm) squares. Cross cut these squares on one diagonal to yield eight half-square triangles from each fabric.

(This amount of fabric will give you slightly too many squares and triangles, but then you have enough different fabrics to be able to shift things around to get your color balance right.)

From the red linen fabric, cut:

• Four 20½-in. (52-cm) squares

• One 43-in. (109.25-cm) square. Cross cut this square on both diagonals to yield four quarter-square triangles.

From the pink-and-yellow striped binding fabric, cut:

• Nine strips, 3 in. (7.5 cm) wide

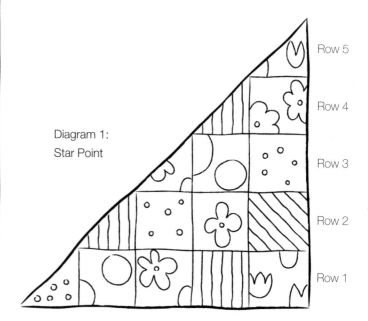

Diagram 1:
Star Point

Row 5

Row 4

Row 3

Row 2

Row 1

Star block

1 Using a bed, the floor, or a design wall, lay out the squares for the center of the star in ten rows of ten squares each. Mix the colors well.

2 Next, lay out the star points, using the photo of the quilt on page 27 as a guide. The bottom row of the star point has four squares and a half-square triangle, the second has three squares and a half-square triangle and so on, until the point ends in one half-square triangle (see Diagram 1).

3 When you have laid all of the fabrics out, stand back and move them around until you are happy with the mix of colors and the spread of the patterns.

4 Begin by sewing the star points together in rows, starting at the point each time and working toward the wide end.

5 When you have pieced all eight star points, press them and set them aside.

6 Piece the star center, also in rows. Press.

Assembly

7 Sew a star point to each side of a background quarter-square triangle with the diagonal edges toward each other, matching the inner points of the V (see Diagram 2). Press the seams toward the star points. The background triangles will be slightly too large for the star points to allow for different people's piecing. When you have sewn the background triangle in, trim any excess fabric on the background triangle to ½ in. (12 mm) above the star points.

8 Repeat with another pair of star points and background quarter-square triangle and press.

9 Sew a star-point unit to the top and the bottom of the star center, taking care to match the seams (see Diagram 3). Press.

10 Repeat steps 7 and 8 with the remaining star points and background triangles and press. Sew a background square to both ends of these last two star-point units.

11 Sew the resulting strips to each side of the star center piece, taking care to match the seams, and press. Your quilt top is complete.

Backing, quilting, and binding

12 Cut the backing fabric crosswise into two pieces, each 2½ yd (2.3 m) long. Remove the selvages (selvedges). Stitch the pieces together along one long edge. Press the seam allowance open and press the backing piece carefully.

13 If hand quilting, tape the backing fabric right side down to the floor or a very large table using masking tape, smoothing out any creases as you go. Lay the batting (wadding) on the backing fabric, with the quilt top right side up on top. Smooth any creases and hand baste (tack) the three layers together, using large stitches and working from the center out. The backing and batting (wadding) should be larger than the top for ease of quilting; don't be tempted to trim them back.

14 Quilt, then bind the quilt, following the instructions on page 136–139.

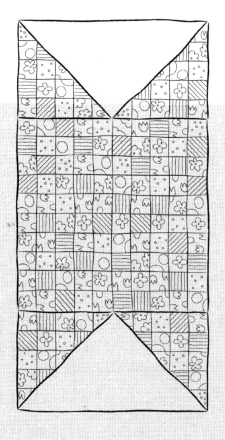

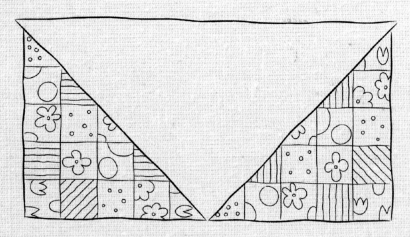

Diagram 2

Diagram 3

Note on quilting
Made in Cherry is machine quilted in a butterfly pattern, using red thread.

Want to scale it down?

This quilt is so sweet made smaller. For a 40-in. (102-cm) square quilt, you will need:

• 6 in. (15 cm) each of eight different prints for the star, cut into 2½-in. (6.5-cm) squares and 2⅞-in. (7.5-cm) squares for the half-square triangles

• 44 in. (112 cm) background fabric, cut into four 10½-in. (27-cm) squares and one 19½-in. (49.5-cm) square

ups and downs

I pieced this quilt at a time when my life was having some ups and downs, as everyone's does. I love the way the duller, textured linen contrasts with the smooth, bright colors of the patchwork fabrics. You can run the zig-zags across the quilt for those days when life is bumpy, or down the quilt when everything is smooth sailing! Either way, they transform some easy piecing into a dynamic quilt.

Finished size

Queen-size (double) quilt, 90 in. (230 cm) square

Finished block size: 9 in. (23 cm)

Material requirements

A wide variety of scraps totalling 4½ yd (4.1 m) or 10 in. (25 cm) each of 20 different fabrics

3¾ yd (3.4 m) natural linen

30 in. (75 cm) blue striped fabric for binding

8 yd (7.4 m) backing fabric

2¾ yd (2.5 m) square piece cotton batting (wadding)

Cotton thread for piecing

Rotary cutter, mat, and ruler

Sewing machine

General sewing supplies

Cutting

From the colored fabrics, cut:

• 400 squares, each 3½ in. (9 cm)

• 100 squares, each 3⅞ in. (10 cm). Cross cut these squares on one diagonal to yield 200 half-square triangles.

From the linen fabric, cut:

• 25 strips, 3½ in. (9 cm) wide. Cross cut these strips into 300 squares measuring 3½ in. (9 cm).

• Ten strips, 3⅞ in. (10 cm) wide. Cross cut these strips into 100 squares measuring 3⅞ in. (10 cm). Cross cut these squares on one diagonal to yield 200 half-square triangles.

From the blue striped binding fabric, cut:

• Ten strips, 3 in. (7.5 cm) wide.

Fabric choices

I used my fabric range, From Little Things, which has 41 fabrics-so the quilt looks very scrappy. To use meterage of fewer fabrics, buy 10 in. (25 cm) each of 20 fabrics instead.

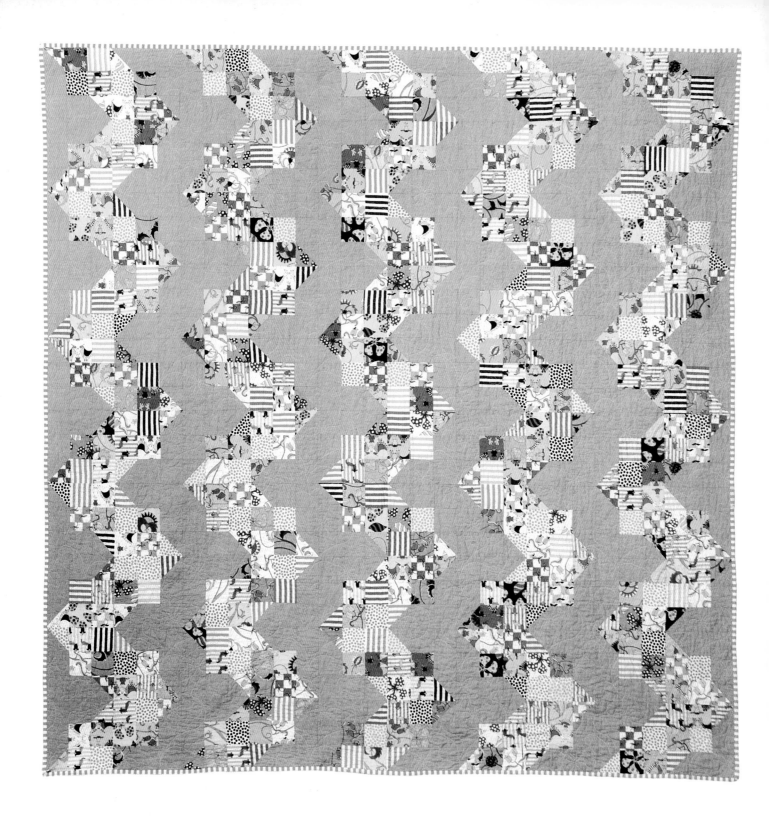

Sewing the blocks

These blocks are basically a very simple nine-patch block, with half-square triangles added. It is very easy to sew in stages.

1 First, stitch a colored half-square triangle to a linen half-square triangle along the diagonal. Repeat until you have 200 squares.

2 Next, sew together three-row units in the following order (see Diagram 1):

Row 1: Two linen squares and one half-square triangle unit

Row 2: One linen square and two colored squares

Row 3: One half-square triangle unit and two colored squares

3 Sew Row 1 to Row 2, and Row 2 to Row 3 to form a square block. Press the seams toward the linen fabric.

4 Piece 100 of each of these blocks, mixing the fabrics well as you go.

Assembling the quilt top

5 Using a design wall (see page 11) or the floor, lay the blocks out in ten rows of ten, referring to Diagram 2 and the photo of the quilt on page 32 for the placement and rotation of the blocks to ensure that you are forming the zig-zags.

6 Stitch the first row of ten blocks together across the quilt. Press all the seams to one side, in the same direction. Repeat with the remaining nine rows.

7 When you have pieced all ten rows, sew the rows together, starting with the top row and working down the quilt and taking care to match the seams as you go, for a neat finish. Press.

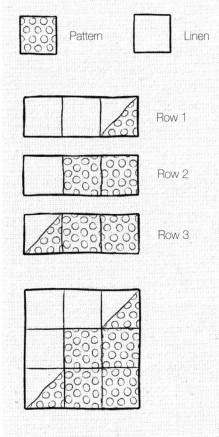

Pattern   Linen

Row 1

Row 2

Row 3

Diagram 1

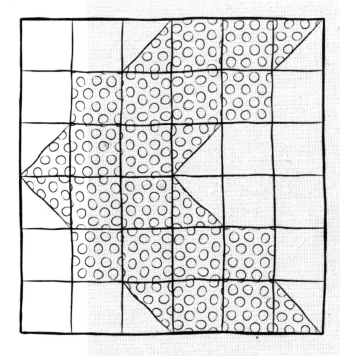

Diagram 2

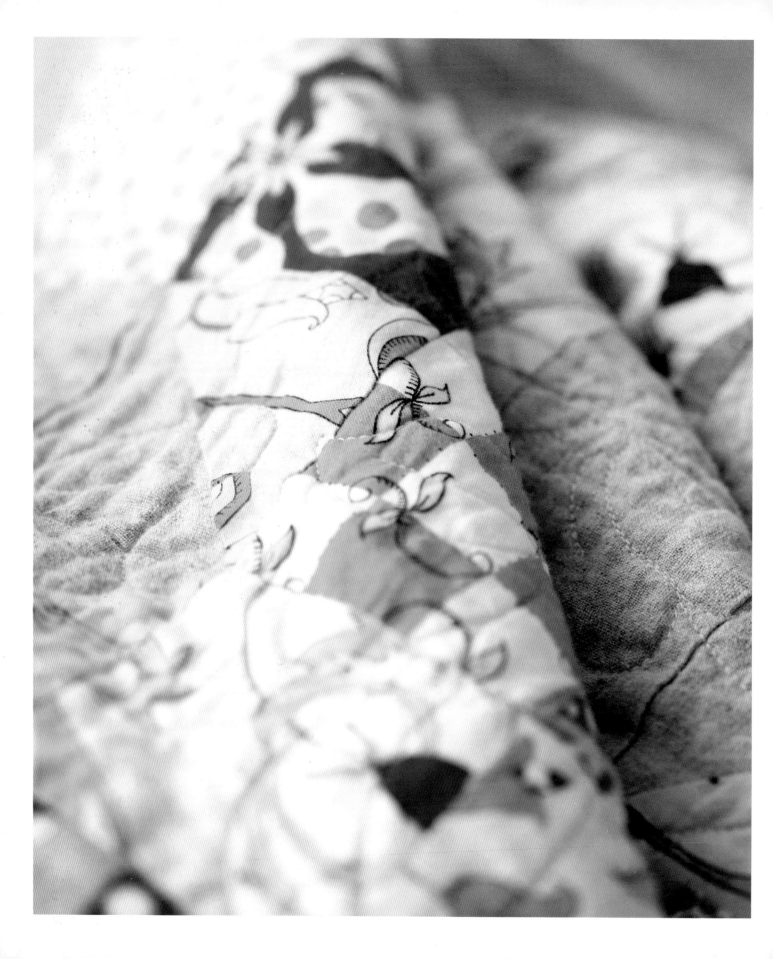

Backing, quilting, and binding

8 Cut the backing fabric crosswise into three pieces, each 96 in. (245 cm) long. Remove the selvages (selvedges). Stitch the pieces together along one long edge. Press the seam allowances open and press the backing piece carefully.

9 If hand quilting, tape the backing fabric right side down to the floor or a very large table using masking tape, smoothing out any creases as you go. Lay the batting (wadding) on the backing fabric, with the quilt top right side up on top. Smooth any creases and hand baste (tack) the three layers together, using large stitches and working from the center out. The backing and batting (wadding) should be larger than the top for ease of quilting; don't be tempted to trim them back.

10 Quilt as desired and bind the quilt, following the instructions on pages 136–139.

Note on quilting

Ups and Downs is machine quilted in an open floral pattern, using white cotton thread.

Want to change the size?

Large twin (single) quilt

63 x 99 in. (160 x 250 cm)

7 blocks across and 11 blocks down

King-size (double) quilt

99 in. (250 cm) square

11 blocks across and 11 blocks down

the bass line
a quilt for Amy

This quilt is very special, and although I designed it, I didn't actually make it. Each block was made for my friend Amy by quilters and bloggers from all over the world. Some have signed their blocks and others haven't.

When Amy's husband Dan passed away in 2011, I wanted to do something for her that would be like a big hug from the blogging community. Amy is much loved the Blog-iverse wide as Mrs Schmenkman Quilts, and I knew there would be plenty of people out there who wanted to help.

I hoped perhaps I would get enough blocks to make a quilt for Amy's bed, and figured I would make more myself if I didn't. I hadn't reckoned on the extraordinary generosity of the quilting community, who flooded enough blocks into my mailbox to make a quilt for Amy's king bed AND her daughter Anabel's bed (shown here), and who also donated the backing, batting (wadding), and machine quilting for both quilts. Craft community magic at work.

I designed the Bass Line block to be like the bass line on a stereo—Dan was a writer who was especially known for his work about techno music. I have included the pattern here by popular request.

Finished size

Queen-size (double) quilt, 70½ x 90½ in. (179 x 230 cm)

Material requirements

Scrap fabric 5¼ yd (4.8 m) or 6 in. (15 cm) of a wide range of fabrics totalling 5¼ yd (4.8 m)

5¼ yd (4.8 m) plain white linen

26 in. (65 cm) blue-and-white spotted fabric for binding

5½ yd (5.1 m) fabric for backing

78 x 100 in. (2 x 2.5 m) cotton batting (wadding)

Cotton thread for piecing

Rotary cutter, mat, and ruler

Sewing machine

General sewing supplies

Yardage (meterage) or scrap fabric?

There are two ways to make this quilt. One is a lot quicker, but will "waste" fabric; the other is slower but will enable you to use scraps and reduce wastage. Instructions are given for both methods; however, both methods will result in some wastage of fabric when the block is trimmed.

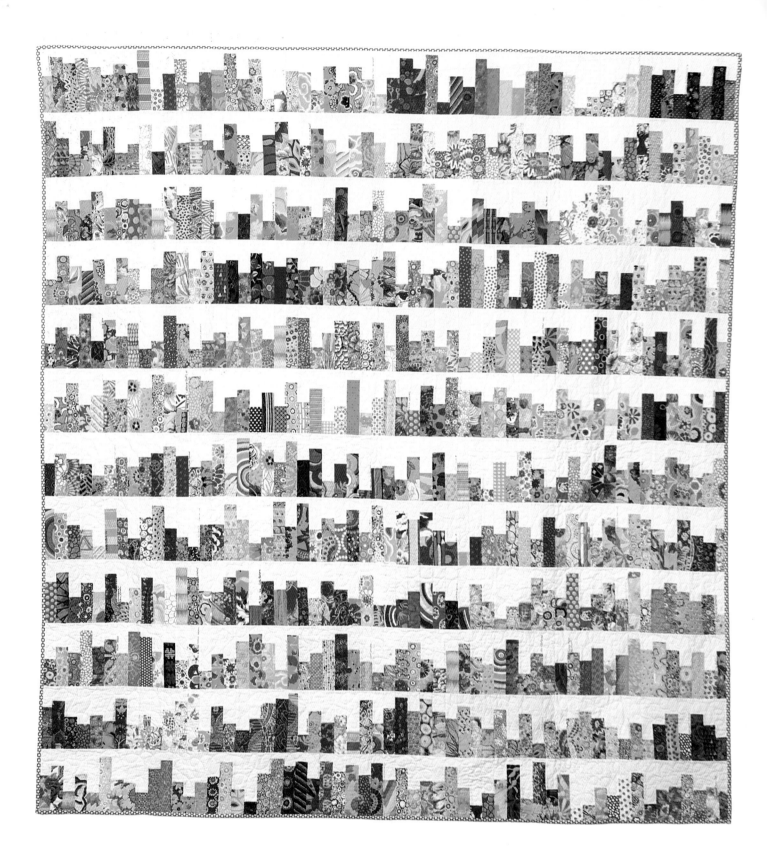

Cutting

If you are using yardage (meterage):

From the fabrics you are using for the bass line, cut a total of:

- Twenty-eight strips, 6½ in. (16.5 cm) wide.

From the white linen fabric, cut:

- Twenty-eight strips, 6½ in. (16.5 cm) wide.

If you are using scrap fabric:

From the scrap fabric, cut:

- 672 pieces measuring 1¾ x 6½ in. (4.5 x 16.5 cm)

From the white linen fabric, cut:

- Twenty-eight strips, 6½ in. (16.5 cm) wide. Cross cut these strips into 672 pieces measuring 1¾ x 6½ in. (4.5 x 16.5 cm).

From the blue spotted binding fabric, cut:

- 12 strips, 3 in. (7.5 cm) wide.

Constructing the quilt top

If you are using yardage (meterage):

1 Sew all 31 pieces of white linen to a piece of colored fabric along a long edge and press the seam toward the colored fabric. Cross cut the strips into 768 pieces 1¾ in. (4.5 cm) wide (see Diagram 1).

If you are using scrap fabric:

1 If you are using scraps, sew a white linen strip to a scrap strip along the short edge and press the seam toward the scrap fabric (see Diagram 2).

2 When you have made all the strip pieces, mix the colors well and begin sewing them into pairs. Stagger the strips as you go, so that the join in the fabrics is in a different place each time (see Diagram 3). The block will be trimmed back to 8 in. when it is finished, so don't step the pieces too dramatically.

3 Sew the pairs into fours, and the fours into eights (see Diagrams 4 and 5).

4 When you have eight pieces in a block, press all the seams in one direction and make sure that the blocks are flat. Trim the blocks to 8 in. (20 cm) high x 10½ in. (26.75 cm) wide (see Diagram 6). Make 84 blocks in total.

5 Lay the quilt out on a design wall or a bed in twelve rows of seven blocks each.

6 When you are happy with the mixture of colors, piece the blocks into rows, beginning with the top left-hand corner. Press all the seams to one side and then join the rows together. Press. Your quilt top is complete.

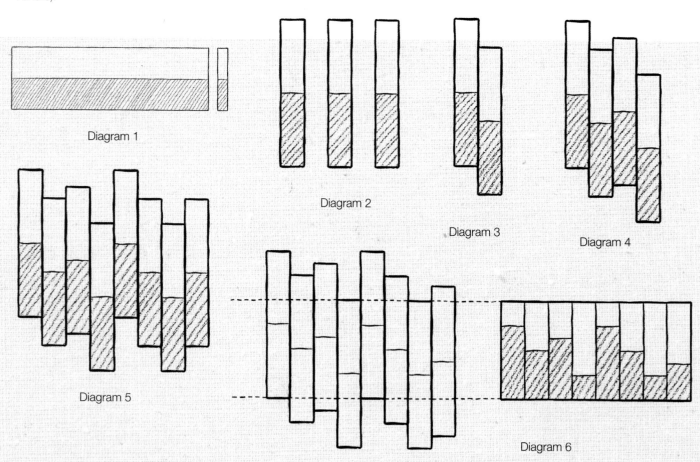

Diagram 1

Diagram 2

Diagram 3

Diagram 4

Diagram 5

Diagram 6

Backing, quilting, and binding

7 Cut the backing fabric crosswise into two pieces, each 103 in. (2.6 m) long. Remove the selvages (selvedges) and stitch the pieces together along one long edge. Press the seam allowance open and press the backing piece carefully.

8 Using masking tape, tape the backing fabric right side down onto the floor or a very large table, smoothing out any creases as you go. Lay the batting (wadding) on the backing, with the quilt top right side up on top. Smooth any creases and hand baste (tack) the three layers together, using large stitches and working from the center out. The backing and batting (wadding) should be larger than the top for ease of quilting; don't be tempted to trim them back.

9 Quilt, then bind the quilt following the instructions on pages 136–139.

Note on quilting

The Bass Line is machine quilted in a loopy pattern, using white cotton thread.

Want this quilt for your bed?

Large twin (single) quilt

60 x 98 in. (152 x 250 cm)

6 blocks across x 13 blocks down

King-size (double) quilt

100 x 98 in. (255 x 250 cm)

10 blocks across x 13 blocks down

love beads

Sometimes quilts just name themselves: to me, this design looks like strings of beads hanging on a dressing table, in front of a mirror. The beautiful feature print was what I used to pick the colors for the triangles: if you look closely, you will see that all the colors are already there, waiting to be found. Using a feature print like this will help you to choose your fabrics.

Finished size

Large twin (single) quilt: 62 x 89 in. (157.5 x 226 cm)

Material requirements:

2⅜ yd (2.2 m) large floral fabric for hexagons

4 in. (10 cm) each of 10 different solid and spotted fabrics for triangles

43 in. (1.1 m) light blue spotted fabric for background and border

24 in. (60 cm) yellow spotted fabric for background

60 in. (1.5 m) multi-colored spotted fabric for background

24 in. (60 cm) multi-colored striped fabric for binding

4 yd (3.65 m) fabric for backing

70 x 98 in. (180 x 250 cm) cotton batting (wadding)

Perle 8 cotton in gray, mauve, pink, yellow, green, and blue for quilting (optional)

Cotton thread for piecing

Template plastic or Sarah Fielke Love Beads ruler set

Rotary cutter, mat, and ruler

Sewing machine

General sewing supplies

Cutting the diamonds and triangles
To cut the diamonds and triangles for this quilt, you can use templates, a 60-degree ruler, or the 60-degree line on your rotary ruler.

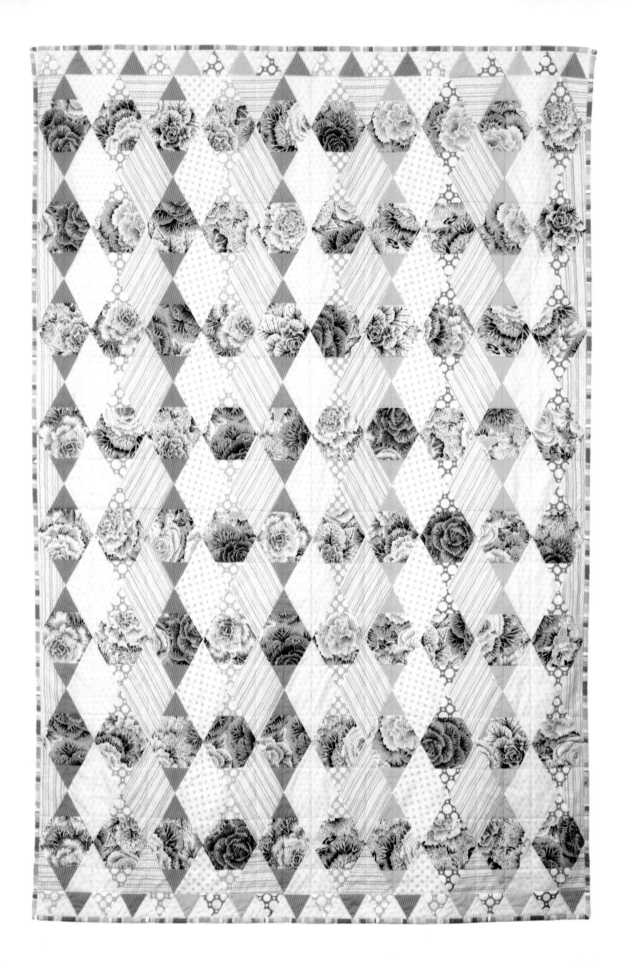

Diagram 1

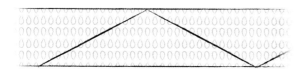

Diagram 2

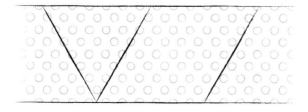

Diagram 3

Cutting

From the template plastic, cut:

One Template A
One Template B
One Template C
One Template D
One Template E
One Template F
One Template G

From the large floral fabric, cut:

• 14 strips 5¾ in. (14.5 cm) wide. Using Template A, cross cut 6 hexagons from each strip to give a total of 80 hexagons (see Diagram 1).

From each of the solid (plain) and spotted fabrics for the triangles, cut:

• Strips 2⅝ in. (5.7 cm) wide. Using Template B, cross cut 20 triangles from each strip.

From the light blue spotted fabric, cut:

• Six strips, 5¾ (14.5 cm) wide. From these strips, cross cut 21 diamonds and six large triangles using templates C and D (see Diagram 2).

• Three strips 2⅝ (5.7 cm) wide. Using Templates B and G, cross cut 38 triangles and 4 half triangles for the border.

From the yellow spotted fabric, cut:

• Two strips, 5¾ in. (14.5 cm) wide. From these strips, cross cut 14 diamonds and 4 large triangles, using templates C and D.

From the multi-colored spotted fabric, cut:

• Eight strips 5¾ in. (14.5 cm) wide. From these strips, cross cut 28 diamonds and 8 large triangles using Templates C and D (see Diagram 3).

• Four strips 3½ in. (9 cm) wide. From these strips, cross cut 14 half diamonds using Template E and four quarter diamonds using Template F.

From the multi-colored striped fabric, cut:

• Eight strips, 3 in. (7.5 cm) wide

Sewing

1 Each "drop" of beads down the quilt has eight diamonds in it that all have the same color tips. Stitch a colored triangle of the same color to opposite ends of all the hexagons, until you have eight diamonds in each of the ten colors (see Diagram 4).

Assembling the quilt top

2 The quilt is laid out in diagonal rows. I strongly suggest you lay the whole quilt out on a design wall or a floor before you start sewing in order to keep the layout of the backgrounds and the colored diamond tips in order. See Diagram 5 and the photo of the quilt on page 44 for placement.

3 When you have laid out all the pieces, begin sewing from the top left-hand corner as indicated in Diagram 5. If you have not sewn diamonds before, it is very helpful to mark the ¼-in. (6-mm) line at the seams on your diamonds before you start to sew. That way you can pin accurately and have a better chance at aligning your points. Sew all the diamonds together in this manner.

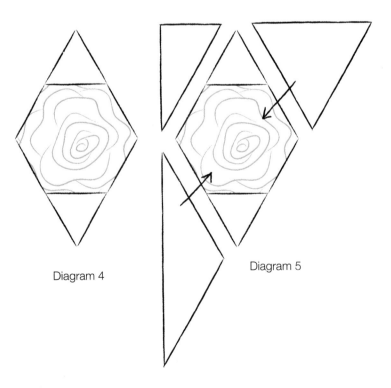

Diagram 4

Diagram 5

4 When you have completed the diamonds, sew together two rows of Template B triangles for the top and bottom borders, alternating between colored and blue spotted triangles and mixing the colors. You should begin and end with a Template G blue spotted half triangle, and there should be 10 full colored triangles in each row.

5 Find the middle of a triangle border and the middle of the top edge of the quilt and pin the two together. Pin the ends, then pin in between, easing as you go if needed. Stitch. Repeat with the bottom border. Your quilt top is complete.

Backing, quilting, and binding

6 Cut the backing fabric crosswise into two pieces, each 72 in. (1.82 m) long. Remove the selvages (selvedges). Stitch the pieces together along one long edge. Press the seam allowance open. Press the backing piece carefully.

7 If hand quilting, tape the backing fabric right side down to the floor or a very large table using masking tape, smoothing out any creases as you go. Lay the batting (wadding) on the backing fabric, with the quilt top right side up on top. Smooth any creases and hand baste (tack) the three layers together, using large stitches and working from the center out. The backing and batting (wadding) should be larger than the top for ease of quilting; don't be tempted to trim them back.

8 Quilt as desired and bind the quilt, following the instructions on pages 136–139.

Note on quilting

I hand quilted *Love Beads* using Perle 8 cotton in a variety of soft colors to match the diamond tips. I quilted straight lines through the center of each diamond running down the quilt and along the seams of the triangles running across the quilt.

Want to change the size?

Queen-size (double) quilt

98 x 99 in. (249 x 252 cm)

16 beads across and 9 down

King-size quilt

102 x 99 in. (259 x 252 cm)

17 beads across and 9 down

Or try setting the diamonds in a different way: you can make a little cot quilt using the same templates and a feature fabric.

millefiori

Millefiori means "a thousand flowers" in Italian—and even though there aren't a thousand flowers here, I think you get the picture! This quilt reminds me of those beautiful little pieces of glassware that people collect. I have a beautiful Millefiori paperweight that a friend gave me, and every time I look into it I am inspired by the colors and shapes. I know all this appliqué looks daunting, but please don't be put off! The shapes are large and easy to manipulate, the curves are gentle, and the spacing need not be precise. Look carefully at my quilt and you will see nothing is perfectly placed—and yet in the scheme of the quilt no one can see it. Just have fun with the colors and forget the rest.

Finished size

Throw or wall hanging, 63 in. (158 cm) square

Material requirements

1¾ yd (1.6 m) lime green linen, 60 in. (150 cm) wide

8-in. (20-cm) square of fabric with a large flower for center circle

20 in. (50 cm) solid (plain) hot pink fabric for center wedges and petals

8 in. (20 cm) pink-and-green fabric for center wedges

12 in. (30 cm) of green-and-white spotted bias tape, or 20 in. (50 cm) of green-and-white spotted fabric to make bias tape

30 in. (75 cm) dark purple lace trim for center

4 in. (10 cm) light blue spotted fabric for center petals

12 in. (30 cm) dark purple fabric for Row 1 hearts

8 in. (20 cm) candy pink fabric for Row 1 petals

4 in. (10 cm) light blue fabric for small circles at base of Row 2 fans

8 in. (20 cm) each of 5–8 different pink fabrics for Row 2 fans

8 in. (20 cm) dark purple fabric for Row 2 large circles

8 in. (20 cm) orange fabric for Row 2 small circles

12 in. (30 cm) dark blue fabric for Row 3 hearts

12 in. (30 cm) hot pink fabric for Row 3 hearts

8 in. (20 cm) light blue fabric for Row 3 small circles

8 in. (20 cm) soft pink fabric for Row 3 large circles

30 in. (1 m) floral fabric for border

4 yd (3.6 m) backing fabric

2-yd (1.8-m) square piece cotton batting (wadding)

28 in. (70 cm) pink striped fabric for binding

Protractor

Chalk pencil

Silver gel pen

Straw needles

Appliqué glue

Hera marker for making bias strips (optional)

Cotton thread to match appliqué fabrics and for piecing

Rotary cutter, mat, and ruler

Fabric scissors

Plastic scissors and template plastic or self-laminating paper if making templates, or Sarah Fielke Millefiori template set

Cardstock or Mylar

Aluminum foil

Perle 8 cotton in pink, purple, blue, green, and yellow for quilting (optional)

Sewing machine

General sewing supplies

Cutting the appliqué fabrics

Using a silver gel pen, trace around the templates. Cut the fabric out ¼ in. (6 mm) from the gel pen line using fabric scissors (see page 129). To cut the circles with Templates A, D, and F, trace onto the BACK of the fabric and then cut out ¼ in. (6 mm) from the gel pen line. This is for making the circles using the foil method (see page 133).

Using Template A, cut:

• One center circle in large floral fabric. (If you want to fussy cut the fabric, hold it up to the light to see where the design is behind the template.)

Using Template B, cut:

• 10 in solid (plain) hot pink

• 10 in pink and green center wedge fabric

• 50 in the assorted pink fabrics

Using Template C, cut:

• 10 in solid (plain) hot pink

• 10 in candy pink for Row 1

Using Template D, cut:

• 10 in blue-and-white spotted fabric for center petals

• 10 in light blue for Row 2

• 10 in orange for Row 2

• 20 in light blue for Row 3

Using Template E, cut:

• 10 in purple for Row 1

• 10 in hot pink for Row 3

• 10 in dark blue for Row 3

Using Template F, cut:

• 10 in dark purple for Row 2

• 10 in soft pink for Row 3

Cutting

From template plastic or self-laminating paper, cut:

• One center circle shape—Template A

• One wedge shape—Template B

• One petal shape—Template C

• One small circle—Template D

• One heart shape—Template E

• One large circle—Template F

Take care to mark them with the appropriate letter, right side up.

From cardstock or Mylar, cut:

• One center circle—Template A

• One small circle—Template D

• One large circle—Template F

From the lime green linen fabric, cut:

• One 54-in. (137-cm) square

(Extra-wide linen in lime green, red, hot pink, gray, and natural is available from my website, www.sarahfielke.com)

From the floral border fabric cut:

• Seven strips, 5½ in. (14 cm) wide

From the pink striped binding fabric, cut:

• Nine strips, 3 in. (7.5 cm) wide

Round and around...

I would love to make this quilt again some
day, and keep going with the pattern to make it
more and more intricate.

Preparation

1 Press the lime green background square in half. Mark this line with chalk. Place your protractor on the line and use it to mark 36-degree angles, as shown in Diagram 1. Rule these 36-degree lines out to the edge of the fabric using your chalk pencil, dividing that half of the background into five wedges. Repeat with the other half of the fabric.

2 Thread a needle with contrasting thread and work large basting (tacking) stitches along each of the chalk lines, taking care not to pull the threads tight and distort the background. You can leave the threads hanging; there is no need to tie them off—they just give you a solid guideline that won't rub off when you place your appliqué pieces in position. Your background fabric should now be divided into ten wedges.

Sewing

3 Sew the solid (plain) pink and the pink-and-green wedges together in pairs along the long sides. Use a very accurate ¼-in. (6-mm) seam to ensure that the wedges lie flat. Sew all the pairs together, alternating the colors, until you have pieced a complete circle. Press very flat, pleating the seams at the center slightly if you need to. Don't worry too much if this happens: your pleats will be covered here by the center circle.

4 Sew all the other wedges together into ten fans of five wedges each in the same way, mixing the colors well.

5 Using a silver gel pen, draw a line around the outside edges of the fans ¼ in. (6 mm) from the edge. The edge of the full circle does not need a line, as it will be covered by the bias edge.

Appliqué

6 Before beginning the appliqué, prepare all the circle pieces following the instructions for making perfect circles with foil on page 133, using the fabric and cardstock/Mylar circles cut with Templates A, D, and F.

7 Fold the floral center circle into quarters and finger press a crease at the edge of the folds. Use this crease to center the circle on the wedge circle. Lift the edges and glue down, taking care not to place the glue too close to the edge or you will not be able to turn the fabric under.

8 When the glue has dried (about 2 minutes), appliqué the center circle to the wedge circle, following the instructions on page 129.

9 Using the basted (tacked) lines on the lime green background fabric as a guide, position the wedge circle in the center of the quilt. Lift the edges, dot glue along the wedges about 2 in. (5 cm) in from the outside edge, and press in place.

10 If you are making your own bias strip, cut two strips 1 in. (2.5 cm) wide from the green and white spotted fabric using the 45-degree angle line on your patchwork ruler. For more information on making bias strips, see page 132.

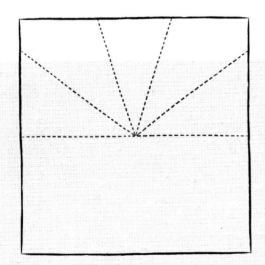

Diagram 1

Diagram 2

11 Position the petals around the edge of the circle, again using the basted (tacked) lines as a guide (see Diagram 2). The petals will overlap each other and go underneath the wedge circle. When you are happy with the placement, lift the edges carefully and glue and then stitch the petals in place.

12 Take the quilt to the ironing board and iron and glue the bias tape in place around the edge of the wedge circle, following the instructions on page 132. When the glue is dry, stitch around the inside edge of the bias circle, through the wedges and into the petals.

13 Tuck the edge of the lace under the outer edge of the bias tape and begin sewing, leaving a tail of lace at the beginning of your stitching to tuck in at the end. You can tuck the lace in under the bias as you go and stitch both to the petals at the same time. When you get back to the beginning of the circle tuck the raw edge of the lace in under itself and stitch down.

14 Turn the quilt over and carefully cut away the fabric from behind the circle and the petals to reduce bulk, cutting ¼ in. (6 mm) in from the stitching line, as explained on page 131.

15 Glue the blue and white small circles into position on the petals. Appliqué the circles in place following the instructions on pages 129–131.

16 Using the same techniques described, position the Row 1 purple hearts between the petals of the center circle, with the pink petals between them and underneath the edge of the hearts. Glue and then appliqué in place.

17 Place the Row 2 pink fans above the purple hearts, with the light blue small circles over the base of the fans. The dark purple circles go between the fans, with the orange small circles on top of them. Glue and then stitch Row 2 in place.

18 Finally, position the dark blue hearts above the Row 2 fans, with the large soft pink circles above them. The hot pink hearts go above the dark purple circles and the small blue circles go in between. Remember that the quilt top will be trimmed to before you stitch on the border, and that there is a ¼-in. (6-mm) seam allowance on each side: do not position any piece closer than 1 in. (2.5 cm) to the edge of the quilt. Stitch and press the quilt top.

19 When you have finished all the appliqué, trim the quilt top to 53½ in. (136 cm) square.

Outer border

20 Remove the selvages (selvedges) and join all the 5½-in. (14-cm) strips of floral fabric together in one long strip. From this strip, cut four pieces 65 in. (165 cm) long.

21 Find the center of one of the strips and the center of the top of the quilt top and pin the two, right sides together. Mark the border 5½ in. (14 cm) from the ends of the border strip, and pin this mark to the end of the quilt top at both ends. Pin in between, easing if needed. Begin sewing ¼ in. (6 mm) from the beginning of the quilt top, and finish ¼ in. (6 mm) from the end. Sew and repeat with the border on the next side. Press toward the border.

22 Using the 45-degree angle on your patchwork ruler, trim a 45-degree angle into the corner pieces of the borders. Sew the corners together up the 45-degree angle and press the seam towards the border. Repeat with the other three corners. Your quilt top is complete.

Backing, quilting, and binding

23 Cut the backing fabric crosswise into two pieces, each 2 yd (1.8 m) long. Remove the selvages (selvedges). Stitch the pieces together along one long edge. Press the seam allowance open and press the backing piece carefully.

24 If hand quilting, tape the backing fabric right side down to the floor or a very large table using masking tape, smoothing out any creases as you go. Lay the batting (wadding) on the backing fabric, with the quilt top right side up on top. Smooth any creases and hand baste (tack) the three layers together, using large stitches and working from the center out. The backing and batting (wadding) should be larger than the top for ease of quilting; don't be tempted to trim them back.

25 Quilt, then bind the quilt, following the instructions on pages 136–139.

Note on quilting
I hand quilted *Millefiori* using Perle 8 cotton. I outline quilted all of the appliqué shapes and quilted a 4-in. (10-cm) grid into the blank corners of the green linen. I used pink, purple, blue, yellow, and green Perle cottons.

made to measure

I am lucky enough to live next door to a man who once owned a beautiful men's clothing shop in Sydney. They made their own business shirts in a rainbow of Italian cotton, the kind of place where you go in and everything is stacked in mouthwatering rainbows of crisp and delicious colors. One afternoon, Dick came walking up our driveway carrying two huge bags, both full to the brim with shirting off-cuts for me to play with. This quilt is just one of the many that I've made from those bags, but I think it's my favorite. Needless to say, Dick has a quilt of his own as a thank-you gift!

Finished size

Queen-size (double) quilt or throw, 80 in. (2 m) square

Material requirements

18 in. (45 cm) deep pink fabric for center block and Borders 3, 5, and 8

3½ yd (3.2 m) predominately white checked or striped fabric for center block and borders 1, 3, 4, 5, 6, and 8

6 in. (15 cm) pink striped fabric for center block and Borders 3, 5, 6, 7, and 8

1½ yd (1.4 m) green striped or checked fabric for center block and Borders 2, 5, and 9

28 in. (70 cm) black striped fabric for Borders 1, 4, 6, and 7

2 yd (1.8 m) purple striped or checked fabric for Borders 3, 5, and 8

4 in. (10 cm) light blue checked fabric for Borders 6 and 9

20 in. (50 cm) yellow checked fabric for Border 8

28 in. (70 cm) brown-and-pink striped fabric for binding

5½ yd (5 m) backing fabric

2¾-yd (2.5-m) square piece cotton batting (wadding)

Neutral-colored cotton thread for piecing

Perle 8 cotton in pink, mauve, blue, green, and red for hand quilting (optional)

Rotary cutter, mat, and ruler

Sewing machine

General sewing supplies

Note

The material requirements are given for each fabric color as a whole, but my quilt is made entirely from samples and off-cuts, so I used several different fabrics for each color: for the white background fabric, for example, I used six different blue- or black-and-white checks, but in the materials list I've given the total amount of white fabric required.

Cutting the center medallion

This quilt was inspired by an antique English medallion quilt that I saw in the Victoria and Albert Museum in London. It is put together from the center outward, one border at a time, and the pattern is written accordingly.

From the deep pink fabric, cut:

- One 7⅛-in. (18-cm) square

From the pink striped fabric, cut:

- Four 4⅞-in. (12.5-cm) squares. Cut these squares in half on one diagonal to yield 8 half-square triangles.

From the white fabric, cut:

- Four 4⅞-in. (12.5-cm) squares. Cut these squares in half on one diagonal to yield eight half-square triangles.

- One 9⅜-in. (24-cm) square. Cross cut this square on two diagonals to yield four quarter-square triangles.

From the green striped fabric, cut:

- Two 4⅞-in. (12.5-cm) squares. Cross cut these squares on one diagonal to yield four half-square triangles.

Sewing the center medallion

1 Sew a white half-square triangle to two sides of the deep pink square and press toward the square. Clip the ears off the triangles and sew two more triangles to the remaining two sides of the square (see Diagram 1). Press.

2 Sew a pink striped half-square triangle to each short side of a white quarter-square triangle (see Diagram 2). Repeat to make four units.

3 Sew two of these units to the top and bottom of the center square and press toward the pink stripe (see Diagram 3).

4 Sew a green striped half-square triangle and a white half-square triangle together along the long edge to form a square and press toward the green fabric. Repeat to make four units.

5 Sew a green/white triangle square to opposite sides of the two remaining pink/white units and press toward the pink stripe. Refer to Diagram 4 for placement of the green fabric.

6 Sew these units to either side of the center square and press (see Diagram 4).

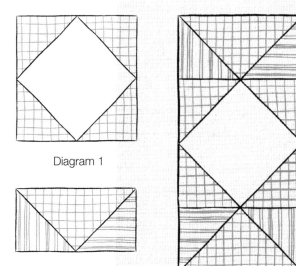

Diagram 1

Diagram 2

Diagram 3

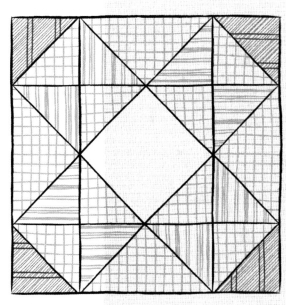

Diagram 4

Cutting Border 1

From the black fabric, cut:

• Eighteen 1⅞-in. (12.5-cm) squares. Cross cut these squares on one diagonal to yield 36 half-square triangles.

From the white fabric, cut:

• Eighteen 1⅞-in. (12.5-cm) squares. Cross cut these squares on one diagonal to yield 36 half-square triangles.

Sewing Border 1

7 Sew a black and a white triangle together along the diagonal side to make a square and press toward the black fabric. Repeat to make 36 squares.

8 Sew two rows of eight triangle units and two rows of ten triangle units, referring to the photo of the quilt on page 61 for the orientation of the triangles.

9 Sew the two rows of eight triangle units to the top and bottom of the center block and press toward the center.

10 Sew the two rows of ten triangle units to the sides of the center block and press toward the center. Press the whole piece.

Cutting Border 2

From the green striped fabric, cut:

• Two 2¾ x 20½-in. (6.5 x 52-cm) strips and two 2¾ x 25½-in. (6.5 x 65-cm) strips

Sewing Border 2

11 Sew a short green striped strip to the top and bottom of the center medallion and press toward the green fabric. Sew the long strips to the sides of the center medallion and press toward the green fabric.

Accurate borders

As this is a medallion quilt, the borders are added one after the other from the center out. It is very easy for the strips to become stretched out of shape as you sew. To prevent this, every time you sew a border onto the center block, you must:

Find the center of the strip and the center of the edge of the quilt top and pin. Then pin the ends together, then pin in between, easing as you go if needed. Then sew. Repeat for EVERY border you attach to the quilt; the extra time you spend pinning will save you unpicking a distorted quilt top later.

Cutting Border 3

From the purple fabric, cut:

• Twenty 3½-in. (8-cm) and two 5-in. (12.75-cm) squares. Cross cut the 5-in. (12.75-cm) squares on both diagonals to yield eight quarter-square triangles.

From the white fabric, cut:

• Twelve 5¼-in. (13.5-cm) squares. Cross cut these squares on both diagonals to yield 48 quarter-square triangles.

For the four stars in the corners:

From the white fabric, cut:

• Sixteen 1½-in. (4-cm) and sixteen 1⅞-in. (4.75-cm) squares. Cross cut the larger squares on one diagonal to yield 36 half-square triangles.

From the dark pink fabric, cut:

• Sixteen 1⅞-in. (4.75-cm) squares. Cross cut them on one diagonal to yield 36 half-square triangles.

From the pink striped fabric, cut:

* Four 2½-in. (6.5-cm) squares

Sewing Border 3

12 Following Diagram 5, sew the short edge of a purple quarter-square triangle to the short edge of a white quarter-square triangle to begin the border. Next, sew the short edge of a white quarter-square triangle to opposite sides of a purple square. Repeat for 5 squares, and then make another triangle unit of a white and purple quarter-squares to end the row. Sew the units together on the diagonal as shown to form the first border strip. Repeat to make four border strips.

13 Sew together all the white and dark pink triangles for the corner stars in pairs along the diagonal side and press the seams toward the dark pink.

14 Sew two of these units together, with the dark pink triangles forming a "V" for the star points. Repeat to make sixteen pairs.

15 With the "V" facing inward, sew a pair of triangles to the top and bottom of a light pink square. Repeat with all four light pink squares.

16 Sew a white 1½-in. (4-cm) square to each end of the remaining eight triangle pairs. Sew these units to the sides of the light pink squares to form four stars (see Diagram 6).

17 Sew a star to each end of two of the border strips.

18 Sew a border strip without stars to the top and bottom of the center medallion and press toward the green fabric. Sew the border strips with the stars attached to the sides of the medallion, taking care to match the seams, and press.

Cutting Border 4

From the black fabric, cut:

• Four 2 x 33½-in. (5 x 85-cm) strips

From the white fabric, cut:

• Four 2-in. (5-cm) squares

Sewing Border 4

19 Sew a black border to the top and bottom of the center medallion. Sew a white square to each end of the remaining two black borders and press toward the black fabric. Sew these strips to the sides of the center medallion and press.

Cutting Border 5

From the green fabric, cut:

• Seventy-two 2⅞-in. (7.25-cm) squares. Cross cut these squares on one diagonal to yield 144 half-square triangles.

From the purple fabric, cut:

• Seventy-two 2⅞-in. (7.25-cm) squares. Cross cut these squares on one diagonal to yield 144 half-square triangles.

• Four 2½ x 36½-in. (6.5 x 92.75-cm) strips.

For the stars in the corners:

From the white fabric, cut:

• Sixteen 2-in. (5-cm) and sixteen 2⅜-in. (6-cm) squares. Cross cut the larger squares on one diagonal to yield 36 half-square triangles.

From the dark pink fabric, cut:

• Sixteen 2⅜-in. (6-cm) squares. Cross cut them on one diagonal to yield 36 half-square triangles.

From the pink striped fabric, cut:

• Four 3½-in. (9-cm) squares

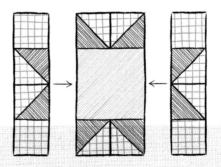
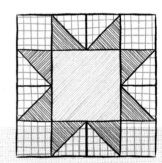

Diagram 6

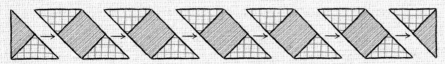

Diagram 5

Sewing Border 5

20 Sew the green and purple half-square triangles together in pairs along the diagonal, then sew the pairs together into eight strips of eighteen squares each. Referring to the photo on page 61, sew one strip of eighteen squares to each side of a purple strip, to make up four Border 5 strips.

21 Assemble the stars, following steps 13–16. Sew a star to each end of two of the border strips.

22 Sew a Border 5 strip without stars to the top and bottom of the center medallion and press toward the black fabric. Sew the Border 5 strips with the stars attached to the sides of the medallion, taking care to match the seams, and press.

Cutting Border 6

From the white fabric, cut:

- Four 4½ x 48½-in. (11.5 x 123-cm) strips. (You may have to join the fabric to do this.)

For the four stars in the corners:

From the blue fabric, cut:

- Sixteen 1½-in. (4-cm) and sixteen 1⅞-in. (4.75-cm) squares. Cross cut the large squares on one diagonal to yield 36 half-square triangles.

From the black fabric, cut:

- Sixteen 1⅞-in. (4.75-cm) squares. Cross cut them on one diagonal to yield 36 half-square triangles.

From the pink striped fabric, cut:

- Four 2½-in. (6.5-cm) squares

Sewing Border 6

23 Assemble the stars, following steps 13–16. Sew a star to each end of two of the border strips.

24 Sew a white fabric border strip to the top and bottom of the center medallion and press toward the white fabric. Sew the border strips with the stars attached to the sides of the medallion, taking care to match the seams, and press.

Cutting Border 7

From the black fabric, cut:

- Four 2½ x 56½-in. (6.5 x 143.5-cm) strips. (You may have to join the fabric to do this.)

From the pink striped fabric, cut:

- Four 2½-in. (6.5-cm) squares

Sewing Border 7

25 Sew a pink striped square to each end of two of the border strips.

26 Sew a Border 7 strip without pink squares to the top and bottom of the center medallion and press toward the black fabric. Sew the Border 7 strips with the squares attached to the sides of the medallion, taking care to match the seams, and press.

Cutting Border 8

From the purple fabric, cut:

- Thirty 4⅞-in. (12.5-cm) squares. Cross cut these squares on one diagonal to yield 60 half-square triangles.

From the yellow fabric, cut:

- Thirty 4⅞-in. (12.5-cm) squares. Cross cut these squares on one diagonal to yield 60 half-square triangles.

From the white fabric, cut:

* Sixty 4⅞-in. (12.5-cm) squares. Cross cut these squares on one diagonal to yield 120 half-square triangles.

For the corner units and stars:

From the white fabric, cut:

- Eight 4½-in. (11.5-cm) corner-unit squares

- Thirty-two 1½-in. (4-cm) squares

- Thirty-two 1⅞-in. (4.75-cm) squares. Cross cut these squares on one diagonal to yield 64 half-square triangles.

From the dark pink fabric, cut:

- Sixteen 1⅞-in. (4.5-cm) squares. Cross cut these squares on one diagonal to yield 36 half-square triangles.

From the purple fabric, cut:

- Sixteen 1⅞-in. (4.5-cm) squares. Cross cut these squares on one diagonal to yield 36 half-square triangles.

From the pink striped fabric, cut:

- Four 2½-in. (6.5-cm) squares

From the dark pink fabric, cut:

- Four 2½-in. (6.5-cm) squares

Fabric choices:

To me, the ice-cream colors of the shirt fabrics are what make this quilt so appealing-it is both modern and traditional at the same time. I love the thrift element, too. When making your own quilt, you could try recycling old cotton shirts, vintage sheets, or tablecloths to get the same effect.

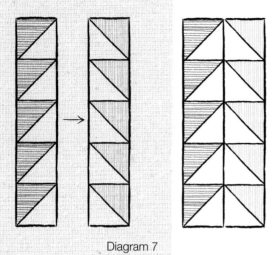

Diagram 7

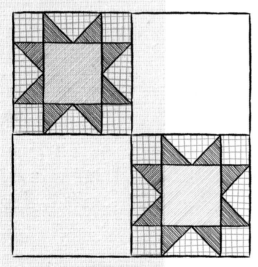

Diagram 8

Sewing Border 8

27 Sew a white triangle to all the purple and yellow triangles along the diagonal edge to form squares.

28 Sew 15 purple and white squares together, referring to the photo of the quilt on page 61 for the direction of the diagonal. Make four rows of 15 squares each. Repeat with the yellow and white squares, making sure that the diagonals face in the other direction.

29 Sew a purple row and a yellow row together, with the white diagonals forming a triangle between them (see Diagram 7). Repeat to make four border strips.

Sewing Border 8

30 Assemble the stars, following steps 13–16.

31 Sew a white 4½-in. (11.5-cm) square to the side of each star, then sew these units together in pairs (see Diagram 8).

32 Sew the corner unit to each end of two pieced triangle borders.

33 Sew a Border 8 strip without corner units to the top and bottom of the center medallion and press toward the black fabric. Sew the Border 8 strips with the corner units attached to the sides of the medallion, matching the seams, and press.

Cutting Border 9

From the green fabric, cut:
• Four 2½ x 76½-in. (6.5 x 194.5-cm) strips. (You will have to join the fabric to do this.)

From the blue fabric, cut:
• Four 2½-in. (6.5-cm) squares

Sewing Border 9

34 Sew the four blue squares to each end of two of the Border 9 strips.

35 Sew a Border 9 strip without blue squares to the top and bottom of the center medallion and press toward the green fabric. Sew the Border 9 strips with the squares attached to the sides of the medallion, taking care to match the seams, and press.

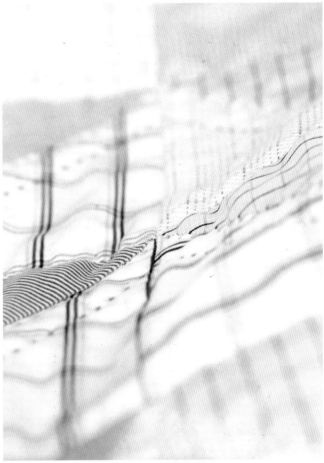

Backing, quilting, and binding

36 Cut the backing fabric crosswise into two pieces, each 2¾ yd (2.5 m) long. Remove the selvages (selvedges). Stitch the pieces together along one long edge. Press the seam allowance open and press the backing piece carefully.

37 If hand quilting, tape the backing fabric right side down to the floor or a very large table using masking tape, smoothing out any creases as you go. Lay the batting (wadding) on the backing fabric, with the quilt top right side up on top. Smooth any creases and hand baste (tack) the three layers together, using large stitches and working from the center out. The backing and batting (wadding) should be larger than the top for ease of quilting; don't be tempted to trim them back.

38 Quilt as desired and bind the quilt, following the instructions on page 136–139.

Note on quilting

I hand quilted *Made to Measure* using Perle 8 cotton in pink, purple, green, blue, and variegated red and purple. I outline quilted each shape in the quilt, ¼ in. (6 mm) inside the seam line.

Want to make this quilt bigger or smaller?

Piecing up to Border 5 only will give you a lovely baby quilt; or you could repeat Borders 6–9 to great effect to make a king-size quilt.

bangles

When I was making this quilt, the patterns reminded me of those stacks of brightly colored bracelets that I had as a little girl in the 1980s. They came in such lovely colors and made that satisfying click as they slid up and down your arm!

Finished quilt size

Large crib quilt or throw, 53½ x 57½ in. (135 x 146 cm)

Material requirements

6 in. (15 cm) each of 24 bright fabrics for bangles

2 yd 1.8 m) white linen for hexagons

3½ yd (3.2 m) blue and yellow floral fabric for backing

1¾ x 2 yd (160 x 180 cm) cotton batting (wadding)

20 in. (50 cm) blue-and-green checked fabric for binding

Cotton thread for piecing

Rotary cutter, mat, and ruler

Sarah Fielke Bangles ruler set or one sheet template plastic

Sewing machine

General sewing supplies

Cutting

From the template plastic
(if you are not using the ruler set), cut:

One Template A
One Template B
One Template C
One Template D
One Template E

Take care to mark them with the appropriate letter, right side up.

From the bangles fabrics, cut:

• Two strips, 2¼ in. (5.7 cm) wide, from each fabric.

• There are six Template A pieces of the same fabric in each bangle. Cut enough Template A in sets of six for 68 whole bangles—a total of 408 pieces. Take care to keep the same fabrics together as you cut.

• There are three Template A pieces in each half hexagon for the top and bottom of the quilt. Cut enough Template A pieces in sets of three for 14 half hexagons—a total of 42.

• There are four Template A pieces in each half hexagon for the sides of the quilt. Cut enough Template A pieces in sets of four for eight half hexagons—a total of 32.

• There are two Template A pieces in each quarter hexagon for the corners of the quilt. Cut enough Template A pieces in sets of two for four corners, a total of eight.

• You should have a grand total of 490 Template A pieces.

From the white linen fabric, cut

• Twelve strips, each 5½ in. (14 cm). From these strips, cut:

• 68 whole hexagons, using Template B.

• 14 half hexagons for the top and bottom of the quilt, using Template C.

• Eight half hexagons for the sides of the quilt, using Template D.

• Four corners, using Template E.

From the blue-and-green checked binding fabric, cut:

• Six strips, 3 in. (7.5 cm) wide.

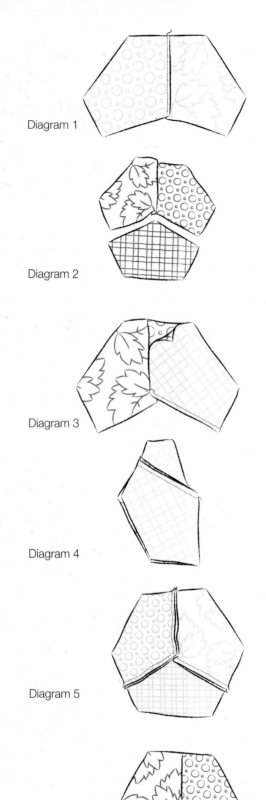

Diagram 1

Diagram 2

Diagram 3

Diagram 4

Diagram 5

Diagram 6

Sewing the blocks

This quilt is not put together in rows, but rather it grows out from the corners in sections. The quilt needs to be laid out in its entirety before it is sewn. To do this, you can use a design wall (see page 11).

1 Using the diagrams provided and the photo of the quilt on page 67 for guidance, lay out all the pieces for the quilt and move them around until you are happy with the placement of colors.

2 When all the pieces are in place, begin sewing the small hexagons together. To do this, you will need to sew an inset, or "Y" seam. Sew two Template A shapes together along the longest pointed edge (see Diagram 1), stopping sewing ¼ in. (6 mm) from the inside edge. Open the pieces out, with the seam pointing to one side, and lay the third piece in the block underneath, so that you can see where it is going to be sewn (see Diagram 2).

3 Place the third Template A piece on top of the left-hand Template A piece and sew from the outside edge into the center, making sure that you do not stitch into the seam allowance (see Diagram 3).

4 When you get ¼ in. (6 mm) from the corner, leave your needle down and pivot the fabric around ready to sew down the next seam (see Diagram 4). Raise the needle and push the seam over, out of the way of the stitches. Replace the needle in the same hole and continue sewing down the other side of the seam. Press the seam down toward the tail of the "Y" (see Diagrams 5 and 6).

5 Repeat until you have sewn all the Template A pieces together into hexagon blocks, picking up the pieces and then replacing them on your design surface as you go so that you don't lose track of where they are supposed to go.

Keeping track

If you don't have an area where you can leave your quilt out while you are working on it, pin your pieces to a sheet or similar and then roll it up and put it away when you are done for the day. That way, all your pieces are still where you left them when you come back to the project.

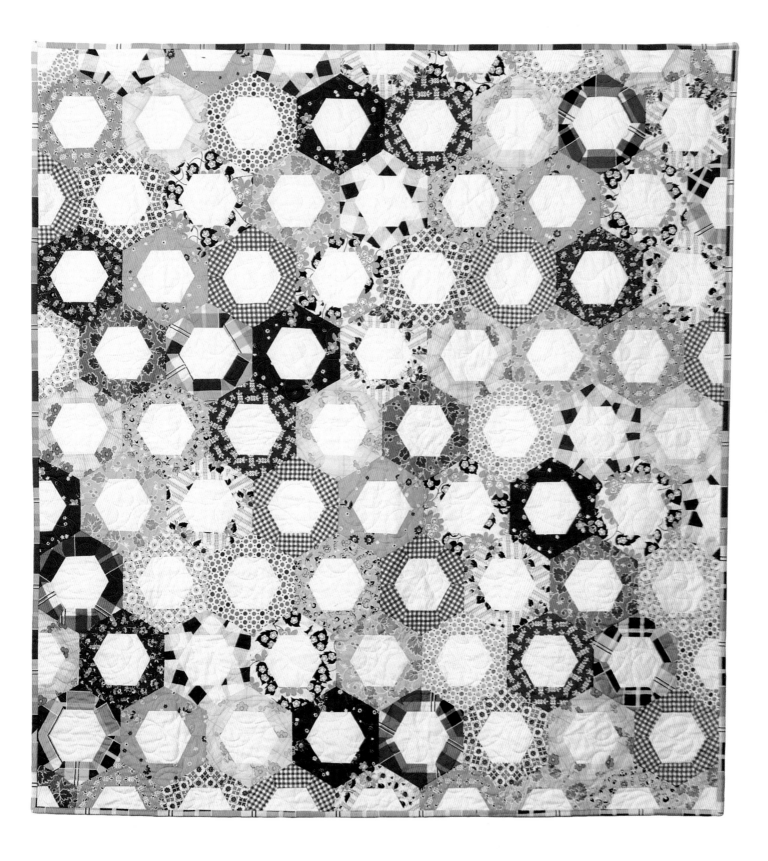

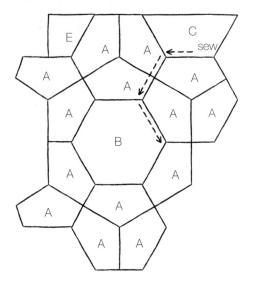

Diagram 7

Assembling the quilt top

6 Following Diagram 7, begin sewing the blocks together from a corner piece, again using the inset piecing technique. (The letters on the diagram refer to the different template shapes, not the color placement of the fabrics; refer to the photo of the quilt on page 67 for colors.) In some places you will have to pivot into several corners to complete a seam. There is no rule on which order they are sewn together.

7 Sew blocks together into larger sections, press the section, then replace the section on the design surface so that you remember where it goes.

8 When you have made a few sections, you can sew those together (see Diagram 8). Don't forget to keep replacing the sections you sew together on your design surface as you go or you will get confused with the placement.

9 When you get to the edges, you will see that some of the Template A pieces stick out from the white setting hexagons. Leave these until the quilt is pieced and then trim them level with the hexagons using your rotary cutter, making sure that the quilt is square (see Diagram 9).

10 Continue until you have sewn all the blocks together and the quilt top is complete.

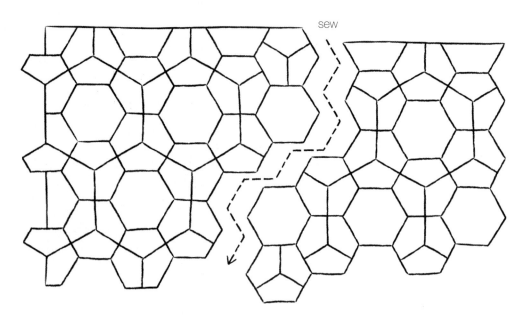

Diagram 8

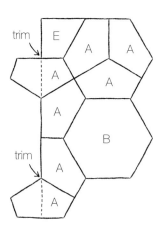

Diagram 9

Backing, quilting, and binding

11 Cut the backing fabric crosswise into two pieces, each 63 in. (1.6 m) long. Remove the selvages (selvedges). Stitch the pieces together along one long edge. Press the seam allowance open and press the backing piece carefully.

12 Using masking tape, tape the backing fabric right side down to the floor or a very large table, smoothing out any creases as you go. Lay the batting (wadding) on the backing fabric, with the quilt top right side up on top. Smooth any creases and hand baste (tack) the three layers together, using large stitches and working from the center out. The backing and batting (wadding) should be larger than the top for ease of quilting; don't be tempted to trim them back.

13 Quilt as desired and bind the quilt, following the instructions on pages 136–139.

Note on quilting

Bangles is machine quilted in a leafy pattern, using white cotton thread.

Want to make it bigger?

This quilt could be easily made larger by making more hexagons and piecing extra until the quilt is the desired size. The measurements for quilts to fit different sizes of bed are as follows:

Large twin (single) quilt
58 x 88 in. (145 x 220 cm)

Queen-size (double) quilt
96 in. (240 cm) square

King-size quilt
100 x 108 in. (250 x 270 cm)

paint by numbers

I made the first star in this quilt intending to make a pillow, but the more I pieced, the more into the idea I got...! Using all the different grades of color is oddly satisfying, like coloring in with a beautiful box of pencils. Pixelating the colors out into the border frames the stars and pulls all the different colors together.

Finished size

King-size quilt, 100½ in. (250 cm) square

Material requirements

Two jelly rolls of Kona Cotton Brights for stars and border (Alternatively, buy 6 in. (15 cm) of at least five tones for each color of star (five greens, five pinks etc).

10 in. (25 cm) each of ten black-on-white prints

2¾ yd (2.5 m) plain white linen

6 in. (15 cm) each of six gray fabrics

1 yd (90 cm) black-and-white spotted fabric for binding

9 yd (8.2 m) backing fabric

2-yd (190-cm) square piece cotton batting (wadding)

Half-square triangle ruler or Sarah Fielke Half-Square Triangle template

Small piece of template plastic if not using ruler

Cotton thread for piecing

Rotary cutter, mat, and ruler

Sewing machine

General sewing supplies

Cutting

If you are not using jelly rolls, cut all your colored fabrics into strips 2½ in. (6.5 cm) wide.

For each star

Referring to the photo of the quilt on page 75 and Diagram 1, separate the five colors for each star and decide where you want them to fall on the star. All squares are 2½ in. (6.5 cm); all triangles are cut from a 2½-in. (6.5-cm) strip, using a half-square triangle ruler or template, or Template A.

Color 1: Cut 8 triangles, 13 squares

Color 2: Cut 8 triangles, 13 squares

Color 3: Cut 4 triangles, 11 squares

Color 4: Cut 12 squares

Color 5: Cut 4 triangles, 11 squares

Cut colors for nine stars and set them aside in color order. Cut all the remaining colored fabric into 2½-in. (6.5-cm) squares for the borders. You will have more than you need, but this will give you a lot of choice when it comes to mixing colors.

From each of the black-and-white fabrics, cut:

• Four strips, 2½ in. (6.5 cm) wide. From these strips, cross cut 510 x 2½-in. (6.5-cm) squares and 108 triangles using Template A.

From the white linen, cut:

• 37 strips, 2½ in. (6.5 cm) wide. From these strips, cross cut 510 x 2½-in. (6.5-cm) squares and 108 triangles using Template A

From each of the gray fabrics, cut:

• Two strips, 2½ in. (6.5 cm) wide. Cross cut these strips into 96 x 2½-in. (6.5-cm) squares and 48 triangles using Template A.

From the black-and-white spotted binding fabric, cut:

• Eleven strips, 3 in. (7.5 cm) wide

Sewing

1 Lay the first block out on a design wall, the floor, or a bed. The five tones for each color of star run diagonally across the star from left to right in the sequence shown (Diagram 1); in the background to the stars, the black fabrics always alternate with the white linen (Diagram 2). Mix the black fabrics well.

2 Sew the star together in sections (see Diagram 3). When you have made all the sections, sew them together in rows to make the star. Make nine stars, using all the different colors you cut.

3 To make the sashing, lay out gray, white, and black pieces in rows, as shown in Diagram 4. Sew the pieces into pairs, and then the pairs into one long strip to make the sashing. Make twelve strips of sashing in this order.

4 Using the remaining gray fabrics, make four 4-patch blocks (see Diagram 5).

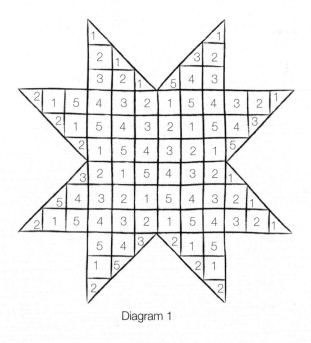

Diagram 1

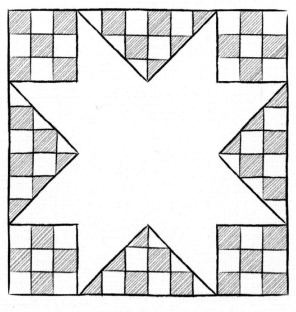

Diagram 2

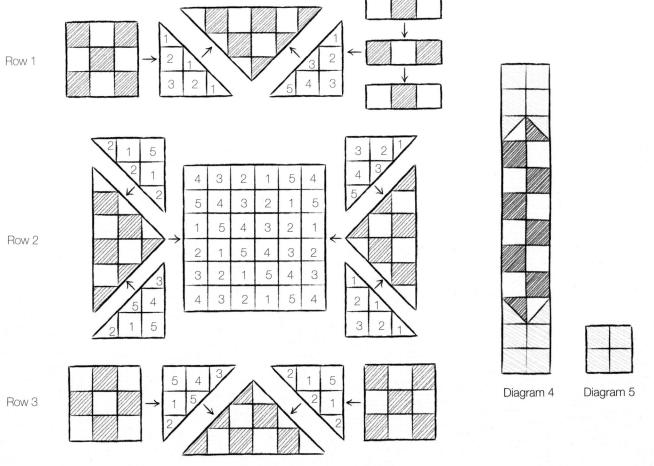

Row 1

Row 2

Row 3

Diagram 3

Diagram 4   Diagram 5

Assembly

5 Lay all the stars out in three rows of three and move them around to decide where you want to place them, using the photo of the quilt on page 75 as a guide.

6 Beginning and ending with a star, alternating stars and vertical sashing strips, sew the top row together (see Diagram 6). Repeat with Rows 2 and 3.

7 Beginning and ending with a horizontal sashing strip, alternating sashing strips and 4-patch blocks, sew the remaining sashing strips together in two rows of three sashing strips and two 4-patch blocks.

8 Sew the three rows of stars together, beginning with Row 1, then a sashing/4-patch strip, then Row 2, then a sashing/4-patch strip, then Row 3. Press.

9 Next make the borders. There is no exact pattern for this: Diagram 7 gives you an indication of placement of color, but you can have fun making your own pattern. The first row (the row closest to the stars) consists of alternating black and white fabrics; the second row has one or two colored fabrics; the third is about 50/50 black and white and colored; the fourth row is almost all colored fabrics with a black or white square thrown in; and the fifth (the outermost row) is all colored fabrics. The top and bottom borders should be 5 rows deep and 44 squares long, and the side borders should be 5 rows deep and 50 squares long.

10 Sew the short border strips to the top and bottom of the quilt, making sure to attach them to the points of the stars. Press. Sew the long borders to the sides of the quilt in the same way and press. Your quilt top is complete.

Backing, quilting, and binding

11 Cut the backing fabric crosswise into three pieces, each 108 in. (2.7 m) long. Remove the selvages (selvedges). Sew the three backing pieces together along their long edges. Press the seams open, then press the backing piece carefully.

12 If hand quilting, tape the backing fabric right side down to the floor or a very large table using masking tape, smoothing out any creases as you go. Lay the batting (wadding) on the backing fabric, with the quilt top right side up on top. Smooth any creases and hand baste (tack) the three layers together, using large stitches and working from the center out. The backing and batting (wadding) should be larger than the top for ease of quilting; don't be tempted to trim them back.

13 Quilt as desired and bind the quilt, following the instructions on pages 136–139.

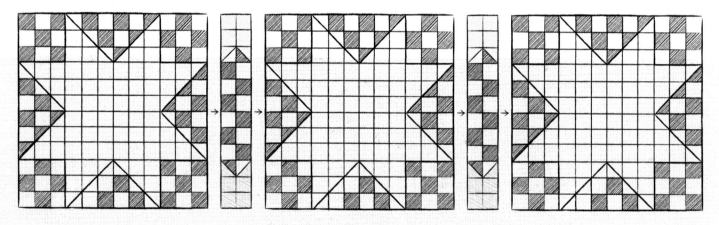

Diagram 6

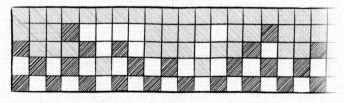

Diagram 7

Note on quilting

Paint by Numbers is machine quilted in a star and loop pattern, using white thread.

Want to make it smaller?

To adjust this pattern to make a queen-size (double) quilt, you could leave off the borders. For a throw, make only four stars with a border. For a quilt for a twin (single) bed, make six stars with a border.

slash that stash

A few years ago, I made a little doll quilt that I use for a class in grading the colors in your stash and understanding contrast. It was fun to make and I have always wanted to make a bigger one. Here it is—with a little crazy piecing around the edge to use up some of that ever-growing scrap pile!

Finished size

King-size quilt, 99½ in. (247 cm) square

Material requirements

A good quilter's stash, and lots of scraps

22 in. (55 cm) tone-on-tone white for sashing

34 in. (85 cm) dark blue fabric for binding

9 yd (8.2 m) backing fabric

108 in. (2.7 m) square piece cotton batting (wadding)

Cotton thread for piecing

Camera or door peeper for balancing colors

Rotary cutter, mat, and ruler

Sewing machine

General sewing supplies

Assessing your stash

Before beginning to cut fabric for this quilt, you need to take a good, long look at your stash. This pattern is a little lesson in what you buy, and why you buy it, and what to shop for the next time you go out fabric hunting.

First, separate your stash into colors, if you haven't already done so. My stash is already color sorted, so making this quilt was an easy exercise. I also have a LOT of fabric, so finding different tones, scales, and patterns wasn't difficult. You can make this quilt with only a small stash of fabrics though, so stand by!

Once you have your fabrics sorted into colors, pick a stack and start there. For each color grouping in this quilt you will need 25 different fabrics—25 green, 25 yellow, 25 orange, 25 red, 25 blue, 25 purple. This isn't as hard as it sounds when you realize that you can include fabric that is predominately one color but has other colors in it, and fabrics that have a white or black base.

Take the stack you have chosen and start looking at the fabrics with a critical eye: you will need as wide and as varied a selection of fabrics as you can get. Don't discard a fabric because it's "ugly"—this quilt is all about the size of the pattern, the saturation of the colors, and the variation of tone.

Looking at your stash by color is also a great way of finding out what you buy regularly. Most people buy fabrics that are predominantly in a medium tone, medium-size print. They also buy pale, small prints regularly—but the majority of quilter's stashes are lacking in dark prints, and in large scale prints. If you do go shopping, consider what is missing from your stash. Lots of light pink and cherry red, but no hot pink or deep blood reds? Lots of small orange prints but no large ones? You may find that you have to purchase some fabric in one color or another, or swap some pieces with a friend! Hunting for the fabric for this quilt should be as much fun as making it, and will also greatly enhance the depth and interest of the stash fabrics you have to work with in the future.

When you have 25 fabrics you are happy with in one color, lay them all out in order along a table or bench, from light to dark. Do it the first time without thinking too hard about it. Then squint your eyes or take a photo of the fabrics and consider that. You will find that, once photographed, the value (tone) of some fabrics looks very different, and that you will need to shuffle fabrics around. There will be some fabrics that will work well in different places and seem to change value wherever you put them; put these fabrics wherever they please your eye the most.

When you have 25 of each color fabric in graded order, you are ready to start cutting. Make sure you take a picture or make a note of your order, so that the fabrics don't get mixed up as you cut.

Cutting

From each piece of each color from your stash, cut:

- Two 3½ x 6½-in. (9 x 16.5-cm) rectangles

From the plain white fabric, cut:

- Seven strips, 2 in. (5 cm) wide

- Two strips, 3½ in. (9 cm) wide. Cross cut these strips into four 3½ x 12½-in. (9 x 32-cm) pieces

From the dark blue binding fabric, cut:

- Eleven strips, 3 in. (7.5 cm) wide

Sewing the graded rows

Your rectangles should be stacked in color grades already, so this is going to be easy!

1 Beginning with the darkest green fabric, stitch 12 rectangles together in order from the left- to the right-hand side of the quilt, and press the seams to one side.

2 For the second row, you are sewing back in the other direction: Row 2 runs from dark to light, right to left. Take the next rectangle in the color sequence and cut it down to 3½ in. (9 cm) to make the half brick to begin the row. Continue sewing along the row from right to left until you reach the last and lightest rectangle. This rectangle should also be cut down to 3½ in. (9 cm).

3 Continue in this manner, following the color sequence as shown in Diagram 1.

4 When you have sewn all 24 rows of the quilt, stitch the rows together along the length. To do this without causing the fabric to buckle, make sure you pin the middle of each row together, then pin the ends, then pin in between, easing as you go if needed. This will help your quilt to lay flat.

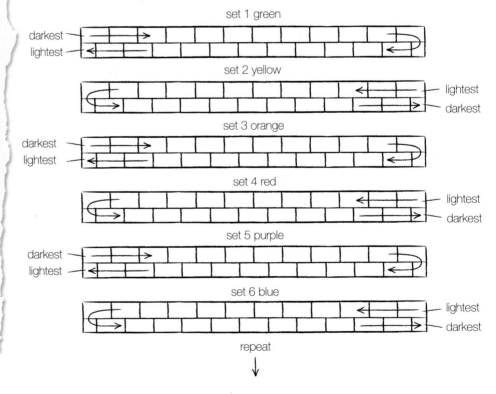

Diagram 1

Crazy patchwork blocks

Crazy patchwork is often done onto a cloth or paper foundation to help keep its shape. I have not pieced onto a foundation: if you are careful about your cutting and pressing, I don't think there is any need, and it adds a lot of weight to your quilt. If you want to use a foundation, cut your foundation squares to 12½ in. (32 cm) and see page 128 for information on foundation piecing.

The blocks in my quilt are all pieced using scrap fabrics. Some of the pieces are large and others small. If you don't have a lot of scraps, I suggest you cut small strips of random sizes off large pieces from your stash; alternatively, ask your quilting or sewing friends if they have any scraps to donate, or buy a bag of scraps from my website to get you started!

Diagram 2

5 Begin a block by taking a piece of scrap for the center of your square and sewing another scrap to it. Don't worry too much about the scraps being straight or the edges being perfect—just make sure that you sew a straight line so that your seams lay flat. Trim away any excess seam allowance to ¼ in. (6 mm) and finger press the seams to one side so that they lay flat.

6 Lay the next scrap right side down at an angle over the first two pieces. Stitch and then trim the excess seam allowance to ¼ in. (6 mm). Repeat until you have a piece of patched fabric measuring at least 12½ in. (32 cm) square (see Diagrams 2–4).

7 Spray the piecing with spray starch and press the fabric with an iron so that it is very flat. The starch will help the block to keep its shape until you are ready to piece it into the quilt. Lay it somewhere flat so that the edges don't stretch. It is very useful to have a block book for this purpose.

8 Trim the fabric to 12½ in. (32 cm) square, and reserve any piecing left over in the trimming to start your next block. Using a 12-in. (30-cm) square ruler is very helpful for doing this.

9 Repeat steps 5–8 until you have made 28 blocks for the quilt border.

Diagram 3

Diagram 4

Note on quilting

Slash That Stash is machine quilted in straight lines across the rectangles using a variegated thread.

Assembly

10 Press the quilt top carefully, and measure it through the center in both directions. It should be 72½ in. (184 cm) square. If it is not, adjust the length of the white sashing strips.

11 Remove the selvages (selvedges) from the 2-in. (5-cm) white strips and sew them all together into one long strip. Cut two pieces 72½ in. (184 cm) long (or the width of your quilt) and two pieces 75½ in. (192 cm) long.

12 Find the center of the top edge of the quilt top and the center of one of the 72½-in. (184-cm) strips and pin the two right sides together. Pin the ends and then pin in between. Sew and press the seams toward the white fabric. Repeat with the bottom edge of the quilt, then add the 75½-in. (192-cm) strips to the sides of the quilt in the same manner.

13 Sew together three crazy patchwork blocks, then a 3½-in. (9-cm) white strip, then three more crazy patchwork blocks. Make two rows like this and attach them to the top and bottom of the quilt as above.

14 Sew together four crazy patchwork blocks, then a 3½-in. (9-cm) white strip, then four more blocks. Make two rows like this and attach them to the sides of the quilt. Your quilt top is complete.

Backing, quilting, and binding

This is a BIG quilt and it needs three drops of backing; however, there will be at least a half width of fabric left over from three drops. To save on fabric, consider using one drop on each side of the backing and piecing scraps of fat quarters up the middle of the backing to get a width of 108 in. (2.75 m).

15 Cut the backing fabric crosswise into three pieces, each 108 in. (2.75 m) long. Remove the selvages (selvedges). Cut one length in half widthwise to measure 22 in. (56 cm). Sew the three backing pieces together along their long edges, with the narrow piece in the center. Press the seams open, then press the backing piece.

16 If hand quilting, tape the backing fabric right side down to the floor or a very large table using masking tape, smoothing out any creases as you go. Lay the batting (wadding) on the backing fabric, with the quilt top right side up on top. Smooth any creases and hand baste (tack) the three layers together, using large stitches and working from the center out. The backing and batting (wadding) should be larger than the top for ease of quilting; don't be tempted to trim them back.

17 Quilt as desired and bind the quilt, following the instructions on page 136–139.

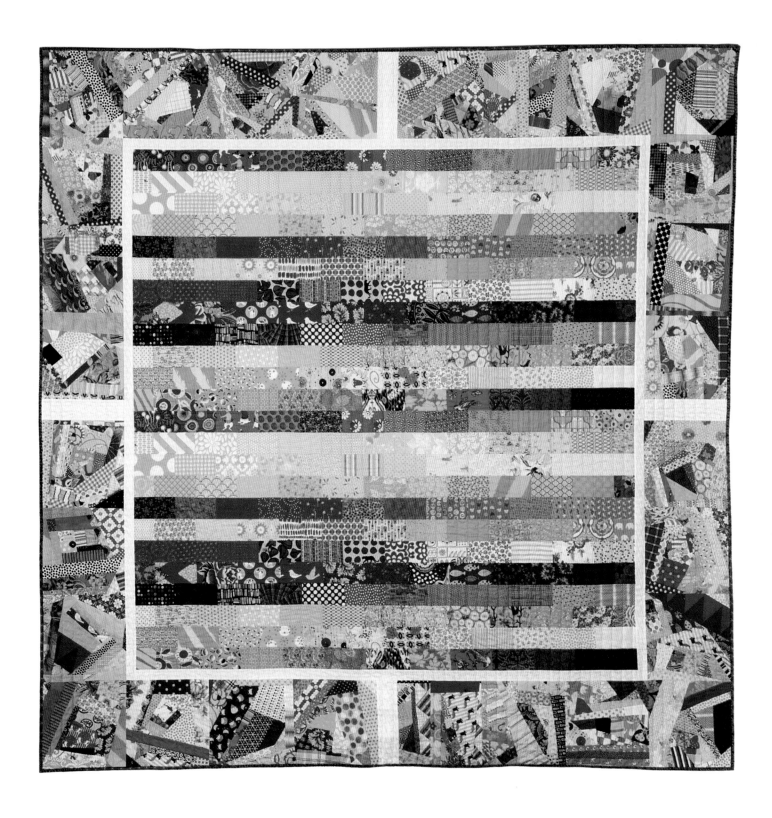

hearts and kisses

When this wide black-and-white stripe came into my life, I just knew something had to be done with it. The appliqué was a pleasure to work and was done in no time. I would love to see this quilt done in a soft palette for a little girl, but right now I think a teenager's bedroom is where it might be headed!

Cutting

From the template plastic or self-laminating paper, cut:

• One heart shape

From the black-and-white striped fabric, cut:

• Three strips, 21 in. (53.5 cm) wide. Cross cut these strips into six 21-in. (53.5-cm) squares.

From the gray-and-white spotted fabric, cut:

• 11 strips, 4½ in. (11.5 cm) wide. Cross cut these strips into 97 squares, each measuring 4½ in. (11.5 cm).

From the kisses fabrics, cut:

• One strip, 6½ in. (16.5 cm) wide, from each fabric. Cross cut these strips into 194 rectangles measuring 1½ x 6½ in. (4 x 16.5 cm).

From the binding fabric, cut:

• Eight strips, 3 in. (7.5 cm) wide.

Finished size

King twin (single) quilt, 60 x 84 in. (150 x 210 cm)

Material requirements

2 yd (1.8 m) wide black-and-white striped fabric

Fat quarter each of two pink, two blue, and two green fabrics for hearts

1½ yd (1.4 m) gray-and-white spotted fabric

8 in. (20 cm) each of seven different pink, green, and blue fabrics for kisses

32 in. (80 cm) multi-colored striped fabric for border

5 yd (4.6 m) backing fabric

2 x 2½ yd (1.8 x 2.3 m) cotton batting (wadding)

24 in. (60 cm) black-and-white spotted fabric for binding

Silver gel pen

Straw needles

Appliqué glue

Cotton thread to match appliqué fabrics

Cotton thread for piecing

Rotary cutter, mat, and ruler

Fabric scissors and plastic scissors

Large sheet template plastic or self-laminating paper

Sewing machine

General sewing supplies

Appliqué

Heart blocks

1 Take the heart template and place it on top of one of the fat quarters, right side up. Using the silver gel pen, trace around both the inside and the outside outline of the heart template. Using fabric scissors, cut the fabric out ¼ in. (6 mm) from the gel pen line. Cut out the center of the heart in the same way. Repeat until you have cut out six hearts.

2 Take a square of black-and-white striped fabric and press it in half horizontally and vertically. Center the heart on the background, with the middle points aligning with the vertical center crease in the background block. The gel pen lines should be 1¼ in. (32 mm) from the sides of the block, 5¼ in. (13.5 cm) from the V-point at the top of the heart, and 2½ in. (6.5 cm) from the bottom (see Diagram 1).

3 Lift the edges of the heart and place small dots of glue along the middle of the piece, not too close to the edges. Press in place.

4 When the glue has dried a little (about 2 minutes), finger press around the whole edge of the heart, inside and out. Thread a straw needle with thread to match the fabric you are stitching and knot the end. Appliqué the heart shapes to the background fabric around the inside and outside edges, following the instructions on pages 129–131.

5 When you have finished the appliqué, trim all the blocks to 20½ in. (52 cm) square.

Kiss blocks

6 To make one Kiss block, take a gray-and-white spotted square and cut it in half along a random line—not on the exact diagonal. These blocks are not supposed to be perfect and the same: they should end up all as different angles (see Diagram 2).

7 Stitch a 1½ x 6½-in. (4 x 16.5-cm) rectangle of kisses fabric in between the two spotted pieces and press the seams toward the colored fabric (see Diagram 3).

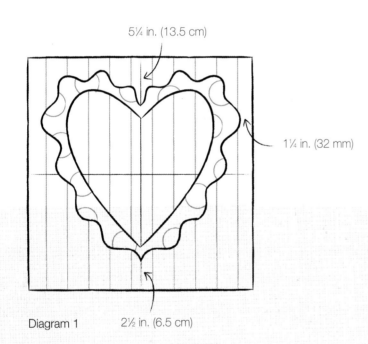

5¼ in. (13.5 cm)

1¼ in. (32 mm)

Diagram 1   2½ in. (6.5 cm)

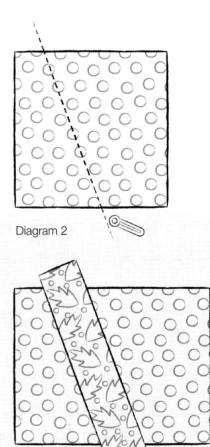

Diagram 2

Diagram 3

Waste not, want not!
Set the cut-out inside hearts aside: you can use them to make matching pillows!

8 Now make a cut through the block in the same manner as before, but on the other diagonal (see Diagram 4).

9 Stitch a rectangle of kisses fabric between these two halves to form the kiss (see Diagram 5). I made each kiss in the same fabric so that they match, but if your quilt is very scrappy you could mix all the fabrics up. Press the seams toward the colored fabric.

10 Trim the block to 4½ in. (11.5 cm) square. You may have to do this on quite an awkward angle: that's fine, so long as the block is square (Diagram 6).

11 Repeat steps 6–10 to make 97 kiss blocks in total.

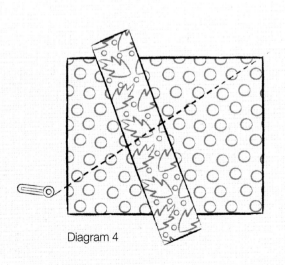

Diagram 4

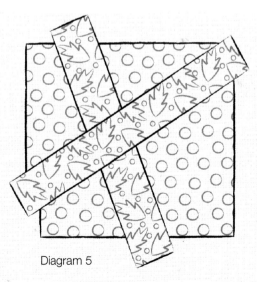

Diagram 5

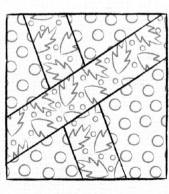

Diagram 6

Want to make it bigger?

Queen-size (double) quilt

96½ in. (244 cm) square

Simply add another row of hearts and kisses and a 6-in. (15-cm) border.

Assembling the quilt top

12 Mixing the colors well, stitch the kiss blocks into 17 rows of five blocks each. You will have twelve single kiss blocks left over. You may want to use a design wall to balance the colors at this point. Press the seams in each row to one side, all in the same direction.

13 Also using a design wall or the floor, decide on which order you want your heart appliqués sewn together in the quilt. Stitch the appliqués together in rows as follows: Vertical kiss row, heart, vertical kiss row, heart, vertical kiss row.

14 Press. Make three rows like this.

15 Stitch the remaining kisses into four rows as follows: Single kiss block, horizontal kiss row, single kiss block, horizontal kiss row, single kiss block.

16 Starting and ending with a horizontal kiss row, stitch all the rows together with the heart appliqué rows in between. Refer to the photo of the quilt for placement.

Outer border

17 Remove the selvages (selvedges) and then join all of the 4½-in. (11.5-cm) strips of multi-colored striped fabric together into one long strip.

18 Measure your quilt top through the middle from side to side and cut two strips to this measurement. Find the center of one of the strips and the center of the top of the quilt top and pin. Pin the ends and then pin in between, easing the fabric as you go if needed. Stitch, then repeat with the bottom of the quilt top.

19 Measure the quilt through the middle from top to bottom and repeat step 18 with the side borders.

20 Press the seams toward the borders. Your quilt top is complete.

Backing, quilting, and binding

21 Cut the backing fabric crosswise into two pieces, each 90 in. (2.3 m) long. Remove the selvages (selvedges). Stitch the pieces together along one long edge. Press the seam allowance open. Press the backing piece carefully.

22 If hand quilting, tape the backing fabric right side down to the floor or a very large table using masking tape, smoothing out any creases as you go. Lay the batting (wadding) piece on the backing fabric, with the quilt top right side up on top. Smooth any creases and hand baste (tack) the three layers together, using large stitches and working from the center out. The backing and batting (wadding) should be larger than the top for ease of quilting; don't be tempted to trim them back.

23 Quilt as desired and bind the quilt, following the instructions on pages 136–139.

Note on quilting

Hearts and Kisses is machine quilted in a spiral pattern, using white cotton thread.

i love all the colors

This quilt was named for my friend's little niece. When asked what her favorite color was, she said, "I love pink, and purple, and red, and blue—oh, I just love all the colors!" I love all the colors, too, and so the quilt got its name.

The separation of the blue and red blocks in this quilt creates a nice secondary pattern, but you could just as easily make this quilt with scraps and it would still look great. The diagonal lines separate the blocks and allow you to play with color in a free a manner as you please. This quilt looks wonderful on my bed, as the appliqué at the top runs along the pillows and the flowers at the bottom drop over the edge.

Finished size

King-size quilt, 102½ in. (260 cm) square

Material requirements

Assorted blue, pink, red, orange, and yellow fabrics for squares

40 in. (1 m) solid white fabric for diagonal grid

14 in. (35 cm) solid lime green fabric for highlight squares

3 yd (2.75 m) aqua-and-white spotted fabric for border

Assorted scrap fabric in greens, blues, yellows, reds, and pinks for appliqué

8⅞ yd (8.1 m) pre-made bias tape in black-and-white check for vines, or 40 in. (1 m) black-and-white check fabric for making your own bias strips

1 yd (90 cm) navy blue fabric for binding

9⅛ yd (8.35 m) for backing

2 yd (190 cm) square cotton batting (wadding)

Silver gel pen

Hera marker for making bias strips (optional)

Straw needles

Appliqué glue

Cotton thread to match appliqué fabrics

Fabric scissors and plastic scissors

Large sheet template plastic or self-laminating paper

Small piece of cardstock

Aluminum foil

Cotton thread for piecing

Rotary cutter, mat, and ruler

Sewing machine

General sewing supplies

Choosing fabrics

This quilt looks best with a lot of different fabrics in it. You will need large prints and small, florals and graphics, lights and darks. If you don't have enough fabrics in your stash, try swapping with friends or buying fat eighths. To achieve a quilt that looks as scrappy as mine, you will need 80 different blues, and 80 different pinks, reds, oranges, or yellows. A 2½-in. (6.5-cm) strip cut across the full width of the fabric will give you enough squares for the outer ring of the block.

Cutting

From the template plastic or self-laminating paper, cut:

- One Template A
- One Template B
- One Template C
- One Template D
- One Template E

From the blue fabrics, cut:

- 16 squares for the outer ring of each block
- 12 squares for ring 2
- 8 squares for ring 3
- 4 squares for ring 4

Cut enough for 12 full blocks and 8 half blocks—a total of 20 blocks and 800 squares.

From the orange/red/pink fabrics, cut:

- 16 squares for the outer ring of each block
- 12 squares for ring 2
- 8 squares for ring 3
- 4 squares for ring 4

Cut enough for 12 full blocks and 8 half blocks—a total of 20 blocks and 800 squares.

From the plain white fabric, cut:

- 16 strips, 2½ in. (6.5 cm) wide. Cross cut these strips into 256 2½-in. (6.5-cm) squares.

From the lime green fabric, cut:

- Five strips, 2 in. (5 cm) wide. From these strips, cross cut 81 2½-in. (6.5-cm) squares.

From the aqua-and-white spotted fabric, cut:

- Ten strips, 10½ in. (26.75 cm) wide.

From the navy blue binding fabric, cut:

- 12 strips, 3 in. (7.5 cm) wide.

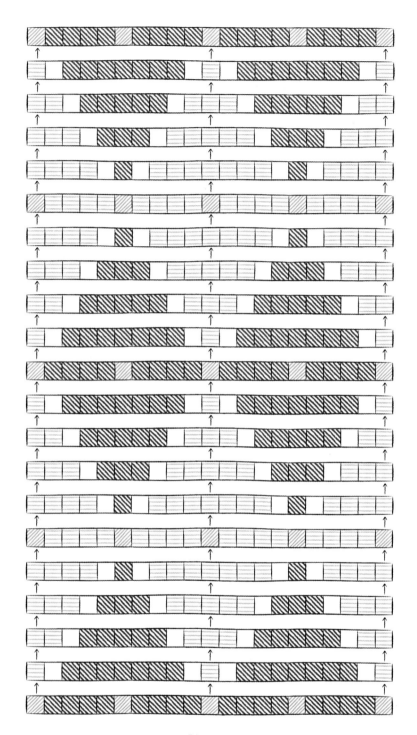

Diagram 1

Tip:
It is essential that you lay this quilt out before sewing it; however, it is a VERY big quilt and it's hard to find a place large enough to lay it out! For this reason, I pieced the quilt in quarters. Lay the quilt out from the top left-hand corner down to 5 lime green squares, and 5 squares across. You can piece this part of the quilt, then lay out the other side, then join the halves, and then repeat with the bottom of the quilt.

Sewing

1 Begin laying one block out on the design wall, the floor, or a bed (see page 11), referring to Diagram 1 and the photo of the quilt on page 90. When the quilt quarter is laid out, sew all the squares in Row 1 together, then all the squares in Row 2, and so on. When you have joined all the squares into rows, sew the rows together, taking care to match the corners.

2 Repeat with the remaining three quarters of the quilt, then join the quarters and press carefully.

Appliqué

3 Your quilt top should measure 82½ in. (218 cm) square. Remove the selvages (selvedges) from the aqua-and-white spotted strips and join them together into one long strip. Cut four strips 102½ in. (260 cm) long. Fold one strip in half to find the center point and mark with a pencil. Measure in 10½ in. (26.75 cm) from each end and mark this spot with a pencil as well.

4 Take the aqua-and-white spotted border to the ironing board begin ironing the black-and-white checked binding into a curvy line for the vine, as described on page 132. Start the curve from just inside the marked 10½-in. (26.75-cm) point at the end of the border strip, and take care to leave a tail of 20 in. (50 cm) of binding to be ironed onto the other border at BOTH ends for the vines to come down the sides of the quilt. Refer to Diagram 2 and the photo of the quilt on page 90.

5 Iron some of the curve, then lift the edges carefully, place a few dots of glue under the tape, wait for it to dry, then press the curve into position on the border. Shift the border along the ironing board, iron another curve, and repeat until you get to just inside the 10½-in. (26.75-cm) mark at the other end of the border.

6 When the vine is dry, lay the border out on a long table or the floor and decide where you would like the flowers in the border to go, again referring to the picture of the quilt for details.

7 From the bias binding, cut five stems for the flowers about 4 in. (10 cm) long. Lift the edge of the vine up where you want the flower to go and place the end of the flower stem under the vine. Glue in place and repeat with the other flower stems.

8 When the stems are dry, use a silver gel pen to draw around the templates on the right side of the fabric and cut:

15 butterflies from the blue scrap using Template A

16 flowers from red hued fabrics using Template B

16 flower centers using Template C

58 leaves from assorted green scraps using Templates D and E

Using fabric scissors, cut the fabric out ¼ in. (6 mm) from the gel pen line.

9 Press the seam allowances of the flowers and the flower centers under with foil, following the instructions on page 133. Prepare the leaves for appliqué as shown on page 129. Set the extra flowers and leaves aside, then position the flowers on the top of the stems of the vine and glue them in place.

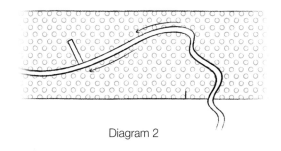

Diagram 2

10 Thread a straw needle with thread to match the vine and knot the end. Appliqué the vine and flower stems to the border, following the instructions for needle-turned appliqué on pages 129–130. Appliqué the flowers to the vine in the same way, then add the flower centers. Position the leaves and butterflies on the border. When you are happy with the placement, glue and stitch them in place (see page 129).

11 Find the center of the border and the center of the top of the quilt and pin the two together. Pin the 10½-in. (26.75-cm) marks at the ends, then pin in between. Begin sewing ¼ in. (6 mm) from the beginning of the quilt top and finish ¼ in. (6 mm) from the end. The ends of the borders and the extra vine at each end will hang over the edge of the quilt top.

12 Using your rotary ruler, mark the top border and the top of the left-hand side border at a 45-degree angle, and trim ¼ in. (6 mm) beyond the marked line. Stitch the top and side borders together along the marked line and press the seam toward the side border. Repeat with the right-hand side border.

13 Take the quilt top to the ironing board and iron the vine curve around the corner and down the side borders of the quilt, almost to the third green square on each side. Referring to the photo of the quilt on page 90, appliqué stems, flowers, leaves, and butterflies to the vine and border, as before. Repeat with the other side border.

14 Stitch the bottom border to the quilt in the same way. Cut seven stems from the bias tape and position them on the border, referring to the photo of the quilt on page 90. Appliqué flowers, leaves, and butterflies in place, as above. Your quilt top is complete.

Backing, quilting, and binding

15 Cut the backing fabric crosswise into three pieces, each 109½ in. (2.78 m) long. Remove all the selvages (selvedges). Stitch two pieces together along one long edge. Press the seam allowance open, then attach the remaining piece of fabric to one long edge of one of the first two pieces. Press the backing piece carefully.

16 If hand quilting, tape the backing fabric right side down to the floor or a very large table using masking tape, smoothing out any creases as you go. Lay the batting (wadding) piece on the backing fabric, with the quilt top right side up on top. Smooth any creases and hand baste (tack) the three layers together, using large stitches and working from the center out. The backing and batting (wadding) should be larger than the top for ease of quilting; don't be tempted to trim them back.

17 Quilt as desired and bind the quilt, following the instructions on pages 136–139.

Want to change the size?

King twin (single) quilt
62 x 92 in. (155 x 230 cm)
5 green squares across and 8 down

Queen-size (double) quilt
92 in. (230 cm) square
8 green squares across and down

Throw
72 in. (180 cm) square
6 green squares across and down

Note on quilting

I Love All the Colors is hand quilted in a diagonal grid across all the squares, and outline quilted around the appliqué. There are lines quilted 2 in. (5 cm) apart through the borders. I used Perle 8 cotton in white, green, navy, and pink.

fancy that

I love a good fan, or Dresden plate, or wagon wheel—after a star, it's my favorite shape in quilting. A wedge is such a versatile shape, and can be assembled in so many ways! Here it's used to great effect to create the swirling shapes of the fans, which are echoed in the machine quilting.

Finished size

Queen-size (double) quilt, 93 in. (236 cm) square

Material requirements

12 in. (30 cm) each of 15 different fabrics for fans, or a wide range of fabrics from your stash

26 in. (66 cm) cream floral fabric for star points

5¾ yd (5.25 m) charcoal linen for background

30 in. (75 cm) dark purple stripe fabric for binding

8½ yd (7.8 m) backing fabric

100-in. (2.5-m) square piece cotton batting (wadding)

Silver gel pen

Straw needles

Appliqué glue

Natural-colored cotton thread for piecing and appliqué

Rotary cutter, mat, and ruler

Plastic scissors and sheet of template plastic or self-laminating paper if making templates, or 18-degree wedge ruler, or Sarah Fielke Wedge Ruler set

Cardstock or Mylar

Aluminum foil

Sewing machine

General sewing supplies

Cutting

From the template plastic or laminate, cut:

- One large wedge using Template A

- One quarter circle using Template B

- One half circle using Template C

- One small wedge using Template D

From cardstock or Mylar, cut:

- One quarter circle using Template B

- One half circle using Template C

Take care to mark them with the appropriate letter and right side up.

From the assorted fan fabrics, cut:

- A large assortment of strips, ranging in width from 1–2½ in. (2.5–6.5 cm). Make sure to keep them in piles of sizes—a pile of 1-in. (2.5-cm) strips, a pile of 1¾-in. (4.5-cm) strips, and so on. Cut different-sized strips from all the different fabrics to give variation. Depending on their width, you will need about 130 strips in total.

From the cream floral fabric, cut:

- Two strips, 12⅝ in. (31.25 cm) wide. Cross cut this strip into four 12⅝ x 17¼-in. (31.25 x 43.75-cm) rectangles.

From the charcoal linen, cut:

- One strip, 34 in. (86.5 cm) wide. From this strip, cross cut one 34-in. (86.5-cm) square.

- Two strips, 12¼ in. (31 cm) wide. From these strips, cross cut four 12¼-in. (31-cm) squares.

- Six strips, 18½ in. (47 cm) wide. Cross cut two of these strips into four 18½-in. (47-cm) squares. Keep the remaining pieces of these strips for the borders.

- Two strips, 12⅝ in. (31.25 cm) wide. From this strip, cut four 12⅝ x 17¼-in. (31.25 x 43.75-cm) rectangles.

From the dark purple stripe binding fabric, cut:

- Nine strips, 3 in. (7.5 cm) wide.

Sewing

Fans

1 Mixing the fabrics well, sew together strips of varying sizes along the length until you have a piece of fabric 15½ in. (39.5 cm) wide (see Diagram 1). Make five sets in this manner.

2 Using Template A, cut 12 large wedges from each set of fabrics (see Diagram 2). You should have 60 wedges.

3 Repeat steps 1 and 2, this time sewing the fabric sets to measure 12½ in. (31.75 cm) wide. Cut 60 small wedges using Template D.

4 Mix all the wedges up well and them sew them along the long side into fans (see Diagram 3). You should make:

Four quarter fans using five large wedges

Four half fans using ten large wedges

Twelve quarter fans using five small wedges

Diagram 1

Diagram 2

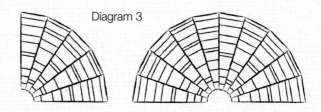

Diagram 3

Tip

When piecing the wedges into fans, take care to use an accurate ¼-in. (6-mm) seam and press the seams to one side. You could use spray starch for stability.

5 From pieces left over from cutting the wedges, carefully trace sixteen quarter-circle Template B pieces and four half-circle Template C pieces onto the BACK side of the fabric using your gel pen. Cut the circles out ¼-in. (6-mm) from the gel pen line. Prepare the pieces for appliqué using the cardstock/Mylar shapes and aluminum foil and following the instructions on page 133.

Appliqué

6 Using your silver gel pen and a ruler, mark a ¼-in. (6-mm) seam along the outer curved edges of each quarter and half fan. You do not need to mark the long straight seams, as they will be sewn into the quilt.

7 Take the 34-in. (86.5-cm) background square and finger press it in half on both diagonals. Place a large quarter fan in each corner of the square, with the straight edges aligning with the edges of the square and the center of the middle fan blade aligning with the finger-pressed diagonal line (see Diagram 4). Make sure the outer edges of the fans meet in the middle of each side of the square.

8 When you are happy with the fan placement, carefully lift the edges of the fan, top and bottom, and place dots of glue on the back of the fan, making sure you do not place any glue along the curved seam allowances that you marked with the silver gel pen. Press in place.

9 When the glue has dried (about 2 minutes), finger press around the outer curved edge of one fan along the gel pen line. Thread a straw needle with neutral-colored thread and knot the end. Appliqué the long curved edge of the fans to the background fabric, following the instructions on pages 129–131.

10 Turn the block over to the back and carefully cut away the background fabric from behind the fans to reduce bulk, cutting ¼ in. (6 mm) in from the stitching line (see Diagram 5).

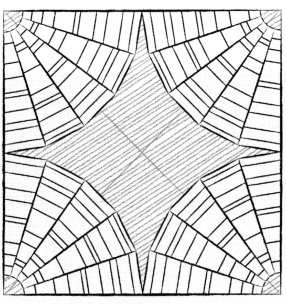

Diagram 4

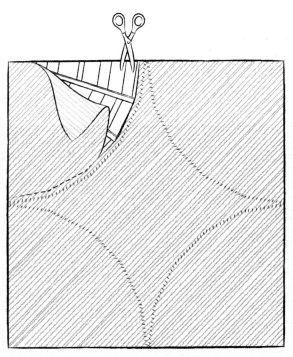

Diagram 5

11 Take the four 12¼-in. (31-cm) squares of background fabric and appliqué one small fan to each square (see Diagram 6). Cut away the background fabric from behind the fan, as in step 10.

12 Take the four 18½-in. squares of background fabric, fold them in half along one diagonal, and finger press. With the straight edges aligning with the edges of the square and the center of the middle fan blade aligning with the finger-pressed diagonal line, appliqué two fans to opposite corners of each block (see Diagram 7). Cut away the background fabric from behind the fans, as in step 10.

13 Remove the selvages (selvedges) from the 18½-in. (47-cm) strips of background fabric and sew them all together into one long strip. From this strip, cut four pieces measuring 57½ in. (146 cm).

14 Fold one of these pieces in half along its length and press. Using the center of one of the half fans as a guide, place the half fan on the border piece and glue in place (see Diagram 8). Appliqué the half fan to the border piece along the long curved edge, as before. Repeat with the other three border pieces and half fans. Cut away the background fabric from behind the fans, as in step 10.

15 When you have appliquéd all the fans to the background, appliqué a prepared quarter circle over the bare corners of all the quarter and half fans. The Template B circles go on the corner of the large quarter fans, the Template C half circles go over the large half fans, and the Template E circles go over the small quarter fans.

Diagram 6

Diagram 7

Diagram 8

Note on quilting
Fancy That is machine quilted, using a variegated thread in a swirling floral pattern.

Assembling the quilt top

16 Take the 12⅝ x 17¼-in. (31.25 x 43.75-cm) rectangles of cream floral and background fabrics, and cut them in half along one diagonal (see Diagram 9). Sew a cream triangle to a background triangle to make eight rectangles, clip the "ears" off the triangles, and press the seams toward the cream floral fabric.

17 Stitch the rectangles together in pairs, with the background fabric making a V-shape (see Diagram 10). Make four pairs of star points.

18 Stitch a pair of star points to the top and bottom of the center square, taking care to match the points.

19 Stitch a small fan block to each end of the remaining two star points, with the tips of the fans pointing outward. Then stitch the star point and fan rectangles to the sides of the center block (refer to the photo on page 100 for placement).

20 Match the center of a half fan border strip to the center of the center block and pin. Pin the ends, then pin in between and stitch, easing if needed. Repeat on the opposite side of the center block.

21 Stitch an 18½-in. (47-cm) square to each end of the remaining two border strips and attach as above, then stitch the resulting piece to the side of the center block. Your quilt top is complete.

Backing, quilting, and binding

22 Cut the backing fabric crosswise into three pieces, each 100 in. (2.5 m) long. Remove the selvedges and stitch the pieces together along the long edges. Press the seam allowances open and press the backing piece carefully.

23 If hand quilting, tape the backing fabric right side down to the floor or a very large table using masking tape, smoothing out any creases as you go. Lay the batting (wadding) on the backing fabric, with the quilt top right side up on top. Smooth any creases and hand baste (tack) the three layers together, using large stitches and working from the center out. The backing and batting (wadding) should be larger than the top for ease of quilting; don't be tempted to trim them back.

24 Quilt as desired and bind the quilt, following the instructions on pages 136–139.

Diagram 9

Diagram 10

string-sane

When I wrote *Quilting: From Little Things*, this quilt was on the design wall in my studio, unfinished and in blocks. I have had so many people email me to ask for the pattern, I knew I had to put it in the next book!

The key to this quilt is to make sure that you have enough contrast between the white fabrics and the blue and pink fabrics. The pattern is subtle, but it's there—the colors radiate out from the center of the quilt in rows.

Fabric colors

The material requirements call for blue and pink fabrics. This is a loose term-except for the Set 1 blocks, which are very blue and pink to make the pattern. The fabrics in the Set 2 blocks, however, are pink and blue with some green, yellow, orange, and red mixed in.

Finished size:

Throw, 73½ in. (187 cm) square

Material requirements

12 in. (30 cm) each of eight predominantly blue fabrics

12 in. (30 cm) each of eight predominantly pink fabrics

18 in. (45 cm) each of four predominantly white fabrics

2¾ yd (2.5 m) solid (plain) white fabric for contrast and border

22 in. (55 cm) aqua spotted fabric for border

1 yd (90 cm) red-and-white striped fabric for binding

4¾ yd (4.3 m) backing fabric

75-in. (190-cm) square piece cotton batting (wadding)

Small piece of template plastic, or Sarah Fielke String-sane template set

Cotton thread for piecing

Rotary cutter, mat, and ruler

Sewing machine

General sewing supplies

Cutting

From each of the blue fabrics, cut:

- Seven strips, 1½ in. (4 cm) wide

From each of the pink fabrics, cut:

- Seven strips, 1½ in. (4 cm) wide

From each of the predominantly white fabrics, cut:

- Eleven strips, 1½ in. (4 cm) wide

From the solid (plain) white fabric, cut:

- 55 strips, 1½ in. (4 cm) wide

- Two strips, 6½ in. (16.5 cm) wide. Cross cut these strips into twelve 6½-in. (16.5-cm) squares. Cross cut these squares on both diagonals into 48 quarter-square triangles for the setting triangles.

From the aqua spotted border fabric, cut:

- Eight strips, 2½ in. (6.5 cm) wide

From the red-and-white striped binding fabric, cut:

- Eight strips, 3 in. (7.5 cm) wide

Sewing

All the blocks in this quilt are cut from two different strip sets. Set them out in the order shown in Diagrams 1 and 2, below, mixing the fabrics well, then stitch together.

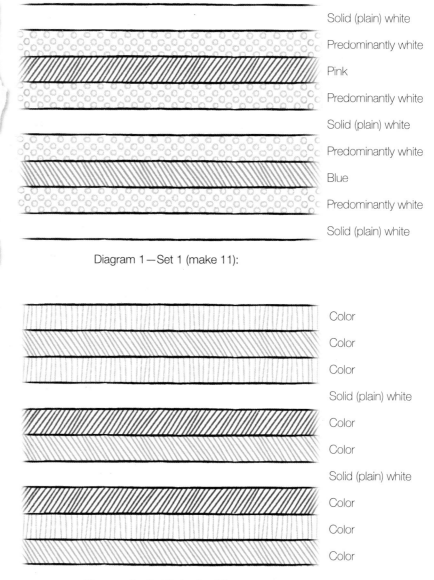

Diagram 1—Set 1 (make 11):

Solid (plain) white
Predominantly white
Pink
Predominantly white
Solid (plain) white
Predominantly white
Blue
Predominantly white
Solid (plain) white

Diagram 2—Set 2 (make 11):

Color
Color
Color
Solid (plain) white
Color
Color
Solid (plain) white
Color
Color
Color

Handle with care!

There are a number of pitfalls associated with the way the pieces for this quilt are cut. One is that you "waste" a lot of fabric. Personally, I don't subscribe to this point of view: it isn't a waste if you are setting out to make a particular quilt, and the triangles left over from cutting out the squares can always be sewn together in another quilt in a different setting. View the extra pieces as an opportunity for another project.

The other drawback is that the squares are all cut on a bias, and therefore will stretch if you aren't cautious. Handle the pieces with care and don't over press.

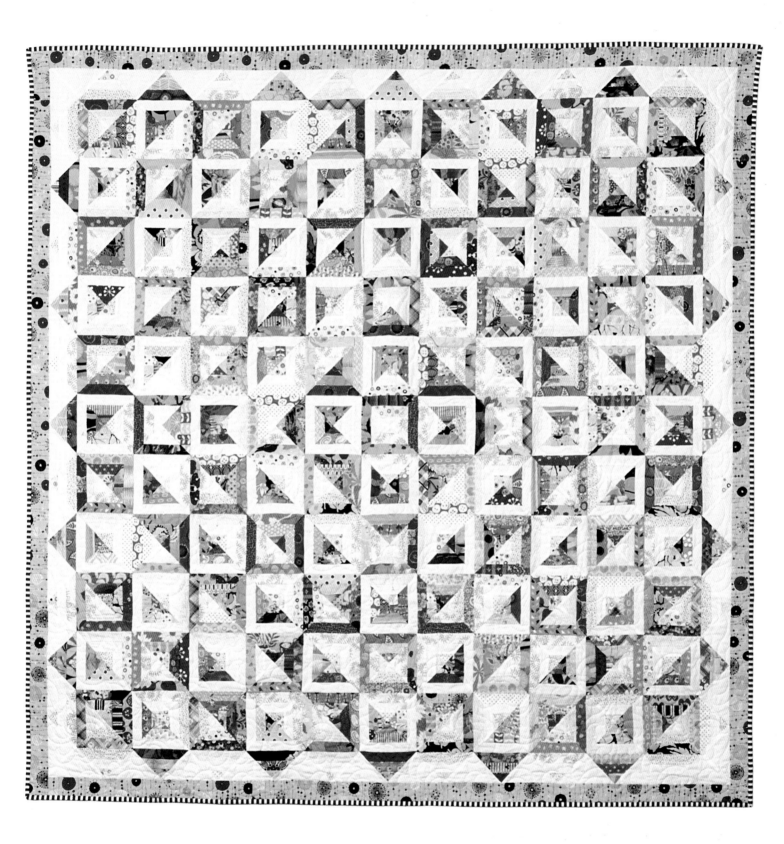

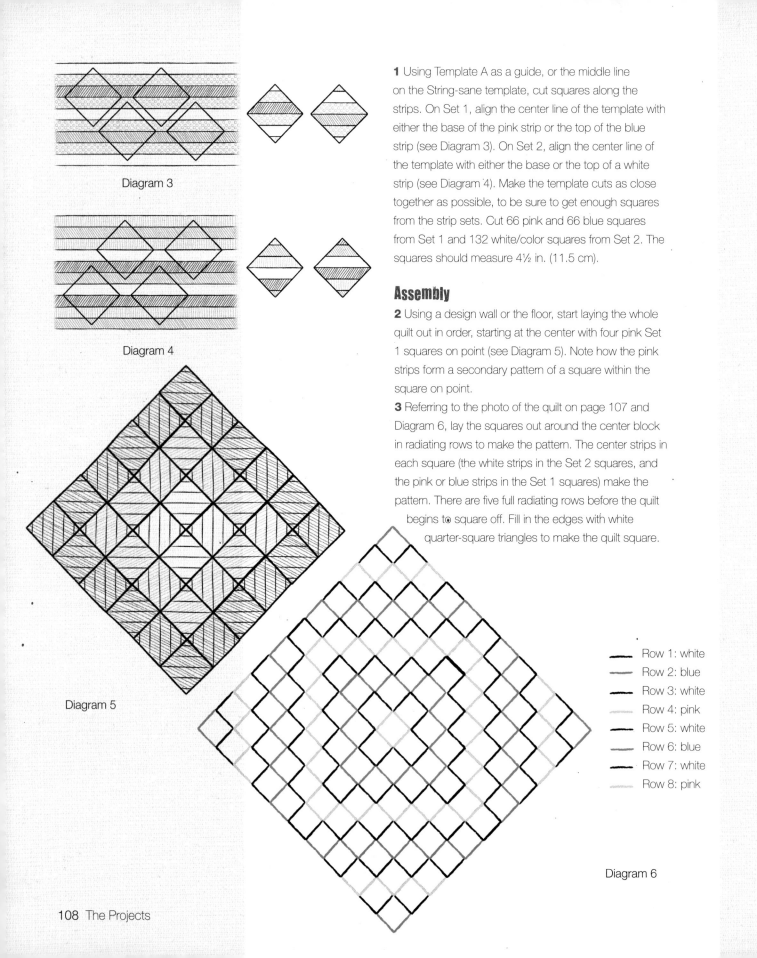

Diagram 3

Diagram 4

1 Using Template A as a guide, or the middle line on the String-sane template, cut squares along the strips. On Set 1, align the center line of the template with either the base of the pink strip or the top of the blue strip (see Diagram 3). On Set 2, align the center line of the template with either the base or the top of a white strip (see Diagram 4). Make the template cuts as close together as possible, to be sure to get enough squares from the strip sets. Cut 66 pink and 66 blue squares from Set 1 and 132 white/color squares from Set 2. The squares should measure 4½ in. (11.5 cm).

Assembly

2 Using a design wall or the floor, start laying the whole quilt out in order, starting at the center with four pink Set 1 squares on point (see Diagram 5). Note how the pink strips form a secondary pattern of a square within the square on point.

3 Referring to the photo of the quilt on page 107 and Diagram 6, lay the squares out around the center block in radiating rows to make the pattern. The center strips in each square (the white strips in the Set 2 squares, and the pink or blue strips in the Set 1 squares) make the pattern. There are five full radiating rows before the quilt begins to square off. Fill in the edges with white quarter-square triangles to make the quilt square.

Diagram 5

Row 1: white
Row 2: blue
Row 3: white
Row 4: pink
Row 5: white
Row 6: blue
Row 7: white
Row 8: pink

Diagram 6

4 When you have laid out the whole quilt and are happy that the pattern is correct and you like the color placement, you can begin to sew. Starting in the top left-hand corner, sew together two quarter-square triangles along their short edges to make the white corner. Now sew the first row of squares, beginning and ending with a white setting triangle (see Diagram 7 and the photo of the quilt on page 107). Continue in this manner until you have sewn the quilt top together. Press carefully, taking care not to stretch the seams.

5 Measure your quilt top through the center in both directions to get the true measurement. It should be 69½ in. (176.5 cm) square. If it is not, take careful note of the measurement.

6 Remove the selvages (selvedges) and sew all the aqua spotted border strips together in one long strip. Cut two strips that are the same measurement as the width of your quilt top. Find the center of the top edge of the quilt and the center of a border strip and pin the two right sides together. Pin the ends, then pin in between, easing as you go if needed. Sew. Repeat at the bottom edge of the quilt and press the seams toward the border.

7 Measure the sides of the quilt, including the top and bottom border strips, and cut two more border strips to this measurement. Attach these strips to the sides of the quilt, as above. Press the seams toward the border. Your quilt top is complete.

Backing, quilting, and binding

8 Cut the backing fabric crosswise into two pieces, each 85 in. (215 cm) long. Remove the selvages (selvedges). Stitch the two pieces along one long edge. Press the seam open, then press the backing piece carefully.

9 If hand quilting, tape the backing fabric right side down to the floor or a very large table using masking tape, smoothing out any creases as you go. Lay the batting (wadding) on the backing fabric, with the quilt top right side up on top. Smooth any creases and hand baste (tack) the three layers together, using large stitches and working from the center out. The backing and batting (wadding) should be larger than the top for ease of quilting; don't be tempted to trim them back.

10 Quilt as desired and bind the quilt, following the instructions on pages 136–139.

Note on quilting
String-sane is machine quilted in a floral pattern, using white thread.

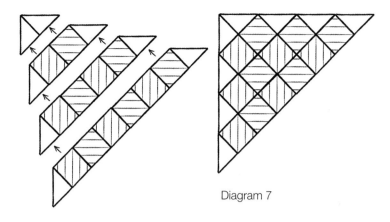

Diagram 7

all that and the hatter

Oh, I love this quilt! I have been planning teapots and cups for ages and ages—but how to do it without being twee? The striped background just popped into my head one day and I couldn't wait to try it out. It's a little mad, but so so happy. It makes me think of all the friends I'd like to have a cup of tea with.

Two fat eighths will make background stripes for two cups or one teapot. It is important to have light, medium, and dark in each color. I used a ColourBox from Oakshott Fabrics. I had a lot of fabric left over, but it did give me a very wide and beautiful range of colors.

There is a fair amount of piecing in this quilt, but it's well worth the effort—and using the Oakshott cottons for the background and Liberty prints for the teapots and cups gives the quilt a silky texture that is a pleasure to hand quilt.

Finished size

Wall hanging, 54 x 60 in.
(137 x 152.5 cm)

Material requirements

Wide assortment of solid (plain) fabrics in fat eighths or 10-in. (25-cm) pieces for backgrounds

27 x 5-in. (12.5-cm) squares for teacups

10 in. (25 cm) each of three fabrics for teapots

8 in. (20 cm) each of six striped or spotted fabrics for the teapot bases and handles

20 in. (50 cm) blue floral fabric for border

22 in. (55 cm) black-and-blue striped fabric for binding

3½ yd (3.2 m) fabric for backing

61 x 67 in. (155 x 170 cm) cotton batting (wadding)

Silver gel pen

Straw needles

Appliqué glue

Cotton thread to match appliqué fabrics

Cotton thread for piecing

Rotary cutter, mat, and ruler

Fabric scissors and plastic scissors

Large sheet template plastic or self-laminating paper

Perle 8 cotton for quilting (optional)

Sewing machine

General sewing supplies

Cutting

From the template plastic, cut:

- One Template A
- One Template B
- One Template C
- One Template D
- One Template E

Take care to mark them with their appropriate letter, right side up.

If you are using fat eighths, I recommend you cut the bigger pieces in these instructions first.

For each teacup

From the cup fabric, cut:

- One 4½-in. (11.5-cm) square.

From the saucer fabric, cut:

- Two triangles using Template A
- One 1½ x 4½-in. (4 x 11.5-cm) rectangle

For Background 1, cut:

- One 1½ x 6-in. (4 x 15-cm) rectangle
- One 2½ x 5½-in. (6.5 x 14-cm) rectangle
- One 1½-in. (4-cm) square
- One 2½ x 1½-in. (6.5 x 4-cm) rectangle
- One triangle using Template A

For Background 2, cut:

- One 1½ x 6-in. (4 x 15-cm) rectangle
- One 2½ x 5½-in. (6.5 x 14-cm) rectangle
- One 1½-in. (4-cm) square
- One 2½ x 1½-in. (6.5 x 4-cm) rectangle
- One triangle using Template A

For each teapot:

From the teapot fabric, cut:

- One 6½ x 7½-in. (16.5 x 19-cm) rectangle
- Two 5½ x 1½-in. (14 x 4-cm) rectangle
- Two 4½ x 1½-in. (11.5 x 4-cm) rectangles
- Two 3½ x 1½-in. (9 x 4-cm) rectangle
- One 2½ x 1½-in. (6.5 x 4-cm) rectangle
- Three 1½-in. (4-cm) squares
- 19 triangles using Template A

From the teapot lid and base fabric, cut:

- One 6½ x 1½-in. (16.5 x 4-cm) rectangle
- One 4½ x 1½-in. (11.5 x 4-cm) rectangle

For Background 1, cut:

- One 13½ x 2½-in. (34 x 6.5-cm) rectangle
- One 7½ x 2½-in. (19 x 6.5-cm) rectangle
- One 5½ x 2½-in. (14 x 6.5-cm) rectangle
- One 4½ x 2½-in. (11.5 x 6.5-cm) rectangle
- One 3½ x 2½-in. (9 x 6.5-cm) rectangle
- Two 2½-in. (6.5-cm) squares
- One 1½ x 2½-in. (4 x 6.5-cm) rectangle
- Nine triangles using Template A
- Six 1½-in. (4-cm) squares

For Background 2, cut:

- Two 5½ x 2½-in. (14 x 6.5-cm) rectangles
- One 5½ x 1½-in. (14 x 4-cm) rectangle
- One 4½ x 2½-in. (11.5 x 6.5-cm) rectangle
- One 3½ x 2½-in. (9 x 6.5-cm) rectangle
- Two 2½-in. (6.5-cm) squares
- Five 1½-in. (4-cm) squares
- Ten triangles using Template A

From the border fabric, cut:

- Seven strips, 2½ in. (6.5 cm) wide

From the binding fabric, cut:

- Seven strips, 3 in. (7.5 cm) wide

Sewing

Cups

For each cup, you will need two different solid (plain) background fabrics. Before you cut the pieces, play around with the background fabrics and the fabrics you have chosen for the main part of the cup and the saucer to see what combinations work well.

1 Using Template B, cut the 4½-in. (11.5-cm) square of cup fabric into a tumbler shape (see Diagram 1).

2 Sew the 1½ x 6-in. (4 x 15-cm) pieces of each color of background fabric to each side of the cup (see Diagram 2). Trim back to a 4½-in. (11.5-cm) square (see Diagram 3).

3 Sew one Template A triangle in each color of background fabric to a saucer fabric Template A triangle to make two squares (see Diagram 4).

4 Taking note of the color placement so that you make alternating stripes of background as you piece, sew the pieces of the cup block into strips (see Diagram 5).

5 Sew these strips together lengthwise to form a cup block (see Diagram 6). Repeat to make 27 blocks.

Note on quilting

I hand quilted *All That and the Hatter* along all the vertical seams, enhancing the stripes, using a variegated perle cotton.

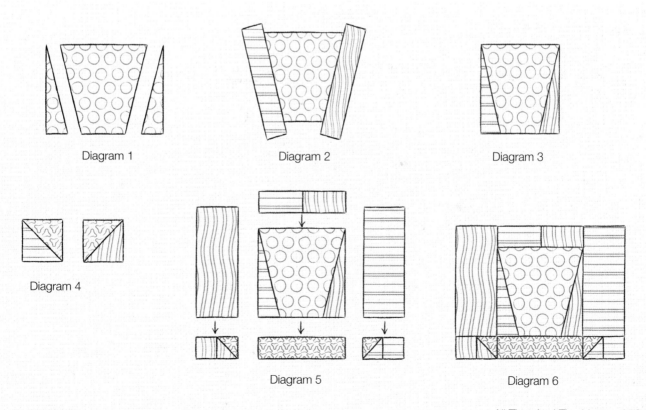

Diagram 1

Diagram 2

Diagram 3

Diagram 4

Diagram 5

Diagram 6

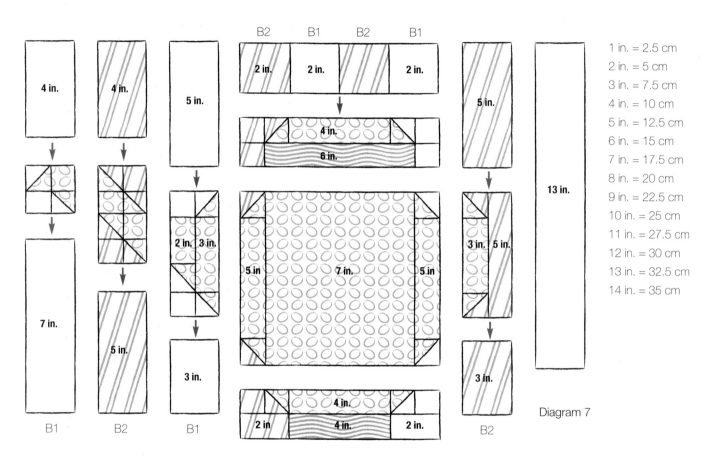

Background 1 fabric

Background 2 fabric

Teapot fabric

Teapot lid/base fabric

Teapots

6 Lay the whole block out before you begin. The teapot is put together in vertical strips, which are then sewn together to form the block. Follow Diagrams 7 and 8 to piece the strips, and then the rows, taking care to pay attention to where the colors go for the stripes. (The measurements on Diagrams 7 and 9 refer to the sizes of the pieces when pieced.) Make 3 teapots.

1 in. = 2.5 cm
2 in. = 5 cm
3 in. = 7.5 cm
4 in. = 10 cm
5 in. = 12.5 cm
6 in. = 15 cm
7 in. = 17.5 cm
8 in. = 20 cm
9 in. = 22.5 cm
10 in. = 25 cm
11 in. = 27.5 cm
12 in. = 30 cm
13 in. = 32.5 cm
14 in. = 35 cm

Diagram 7

Keeping track

There are a lot of small pieces in the teapot blocks. I recommend you make yourself a block board by covering a large piece of card with batting (wadding). Then you can lay the block out completely on the board and take it back and forth with you to the iron, or put it safely away to work on next time without losing any pieces. You can also pick things up and put them down easily without getting your piecing confused.

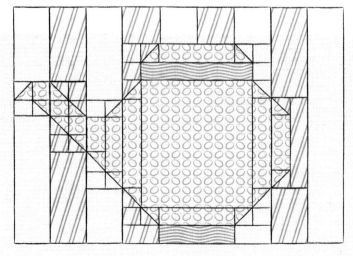

Diagram 8

□ 1 small square = 1 in. (2.5 cm) when stitched

Appliqué

7 When you have made all the cups and pots, take Template C and place it on the right side of one of the cup handle fabrics, right side up. Using the silver gel pen, trace around the template. Cut the fabric out ¼ in. (6 mm) from the gel pen line, using fabric scissors.

8 To begin the appliqué, take a cup with the saucer fabric matching the handle you cut out and line it up on the right-hand edge of the cup, using the photo of the quilt as a guide. Lift the edges of the

handle and place small dots of glue along the middle of the piece, not too close to the edges. Press in place.

9 When the glue has dried (about 2 minutes), finger press around the whole edge of the handle, inside and out. Following the instruction for needle-turn appliqué on page 129, appliqué the handle to the cup, starting with the inside of the handle, then the outer edge, and finally the edges touching the cup.

10 Repeat with all the cups, the teapot handles, and the tops of the teapot lids.

Assembly

11 Following Diagram 9 carefully, lay all the blocks out on a design wall or a table without cutting any of the filler pieces. Once you have all of the cups and pots in the right place color-wise, then begin cutting the filler pieces. This enables you to see where you have put the background colors and to mix the colors accordingly. Refer to Diagram 9 for the sizes of the background fabric filler pieces you need to cut, adding ¼ in. (6 mm) to each edge all around each piece to allow for the seam allowances.

Each section of the quilt will be pieced as a small block before it goes into the main quilt, as shown in Diagram 9. This is because there are partial seams involved in some of the stitching; where to leave the seams partially open is indicated by the small red dots on the diagram. (For information on partial seams, see page 127.)

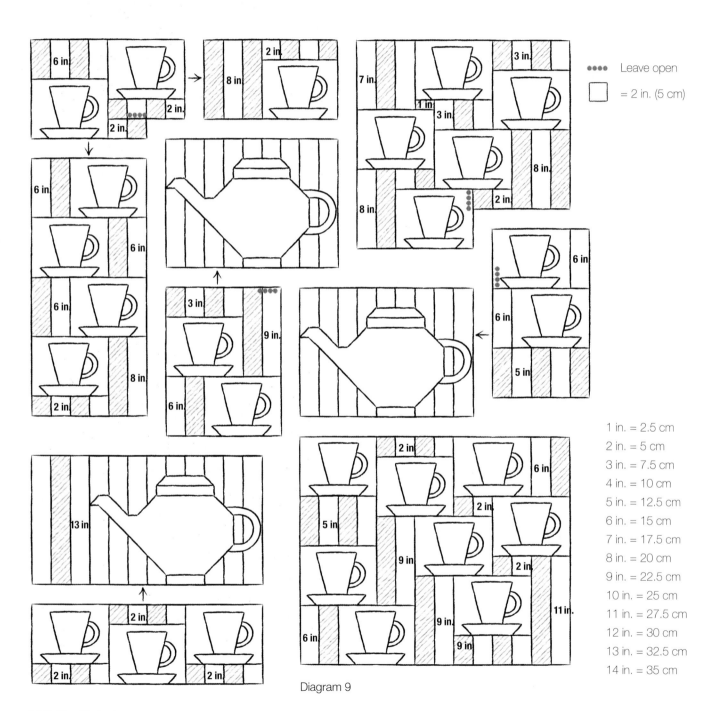

•••• Leave open

□ = 2 in. (5 cm)

1 in. = 2.5 cm
2 in. = 5 cm
3 in. = 7.5 cm
4 in. = 10 cm
5 in. = 12.5 cm
6 in. = 15 cm
7 in. = 17.5 cm
8 in. = 20 cm
9 in. = 22.5 cm
10 in. = 25 cm
11 in. = 27.5 cm
12 in. = 30 cm
13 in. = 32.5 cm
14 in. = 35 cm

Diagram 9

12 When you have sewn the block sections together, follow Diagrams 10–12 to stitch the blocks into larger sections.

13 Remove the selvages (selvedges) from the seven border strips and sew them all together into one long strip. Measure your quilt top through the center from side to side. Cut two strips from the border fabric to this measurement. Find the middle of the top edge of the quilt top and the middle of a border strip and pin. Pin the ends, then pin in between and ease as you go if needed. Stitch. Repeat with the bottom border.

14 Measure your quilt top through the center from top to bottom. Cut two strips from the border fabric to this measurement. Find the middle of the left-hand side of the quilt top and the middle of a border strip and pin. Pin the ends, then pin in between and ease as you go if needed. Stitch. Repeat with the right-hand side border. Your quilt top is complete.

Backing, quilting, and binding

15 Cut the backing fabric carefully into two pieces 63 in. (1.55 m) long. Remove the selvages (selvedges). Stitch the two pieces along one long edge. Press the seam allowance open, then press the backing piece carefully.

16 If hand quilting, tape the backing fabric right side down to the floor or a very large table using masking tape, smoothing out any creases as you go. Lay the batting (wadding) on the backing fabric, with the quilt top right side up on top. Smooth any creases and hand baste (tack) the three layers together, using large stitches and working from the center out. The backing and batting (wadding) should be larger than the top for ease of quilting; don't be tempted to trim them back.

17 Quilt as desired and bind the quilt, following the instructions on page 136–139.

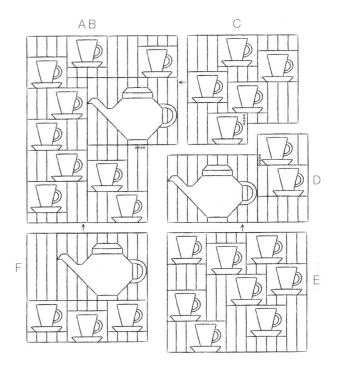

Diagram 11

Diagram 12

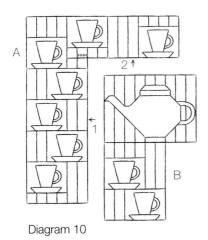

Diagram 10

lady marmalade

This quilt began with the gray-and-marmalade striped fabric in the center square. It's a piece of an antique feedsack, given to me by a friend. The colors took my fancy and I started playing with it as an appliqué background. As it was vintage I only had a small piece and no way of getting any more, so the quilt just grew out from the center and I found other pieces to go into it as I went. One of my favorite things about this quilt is all the animal prints in the appliqué circles, they make me smile every time I look at it.

Finished size

Throw, 67½ in. (169 cm) square

Material requirements

Scrap of eggplant floral fabric for heart

Fat quarter each of green floral and pink floral fabric for center panel

10 in. (25 cm) yellow fabric for star points

Fat quarter of gray-and-orange striped fabric for center background

10 in. (25 cm) blue floral fabric for center circle and Border 1

12 in. (30 cm) multi-colored striped fabric for Border 2

70 x 5-in. (12.5-cm) patterned squares for Borders 1, 3, and 5

10 in. (25 cm) light blue fabric for Border 4

4 in. (10 cm) each of seven blue fabrics for Border 5 pieced blocks

2 in. (5 cm) each of 10 pink and yellow fabrics for Border 5 pieced blocks

14 in. (35 cm) red patterned fabric for Border 5 setting triangles

12 in. (30 cm) hot pink fabric for Border 5 flowers

8 in. (20 cm) light blue fabric for Border 5 flower centers

12 in. (30 cm) light green floral fabric for Border 6

28 in. (70 cm) multi-colored floral fabric for Border 7

2½ yd (2.3 m) solid eggplant fabric for background

24 in. (60 cm) blue fabric for binding

4⅜ yd (4 m) backing fabric

76-in. (1.9-m) square piece cotton batting (wadding)

Silver gel pen

Straw needles

Appliqué glue

Cotton thread to match appliqué fabrics

Cotton thread for piecing

Rotary cutter, mat, and ruler

Fabric scissors and plastic scissors

Two sheets template plastic or self-laminating paper

Cardstock

Aluminum foil

Perle 8 cotton in dark gray, pink, and mauve for quilting (optional)

Sewing machine

General sewing supplies

Cutting

From the template plastic or self-laminating paper, cut:

- One Template A heart
- One Template B circle
- One Template C flower
- One Template D circle
- One Template E quarter circle
- One Template F triangle
- One Template G quarter circle
- One Template H jagged border
- One Template I circle
- One Template J circle
- One Template K triangle

Take care to mark them with the appropriate letter, right side up.

From the gray-and-orange striped fabric, cut:

- One 17-in. (43-cm) square

From the multi-colored striped Border 2 fabric, cut:

- Four 2¾ x 30-in. (7 x 76-cm) strips

From the light blue Border 4 fabric, cut:

- Four 2 x 43-in. (5 x 109.25-cm) strips

From each of the seven blue Border 5 fabrics, cut:

- One strip, 2⅞ in. (7.25 cm) wide. Cross cut this strip into two 2⅞-in. (7.25-cm) squares. Cross cut each of these squares in half on one diagonal to form half-square triangles.

- Cut the remaining part of this strip down to 1⅞ in. (4.75 cm). Cross cut this strip into six 1⅞-in. (4.75-cm) squares. Cross cut these squares in half on one diagonal to yield 12 half-square triangles.

From the red setting Border 5 fabric, cut:

- One strip, 6¾ in. (17 cm) wide. Cross cut this strip into six 6¾-in. (17-cm) squares. Cross cut these squares on both diagonals to form 24 setting triangles.

- One strip, 4⅞ in. (12.5 cm) wide. Cross cut this strip into four 4⅞-in. (12.5-cm) squares. Cross cut these squares on one diagonal to form half-square triangles for the ends of the rows.

From the pink and yellow Border 5 fabrics, cut:

- Ten strips, 1¾ in. (4.5 cm) wide

From the green floral Border 6 fabric, cut:

- Six 2-in. (5-cm) strips

From the multi-colored floral Border 7 fabric, cut:

- Six strips, 4½ in. (11.5 cm) wide for the outer border

From the solid (plain) eggplant fabric, cut:

- Nine strips, 4½ in. (11.5 cm) wide. From these strips, cross cut 64 x 4½-in. (11.5-cm) squares for Borders 1, 3, 7, and 7 and four pieces measuring 4½ x 17 in. (11.5 x 43 cm) for Border 1.

- One strip, 8¾ in. (22.25 cm) wide. From this strip, cut four 8¾-in. (22.25-cm) squares for the corners of Border 5.

- Six strips, 1⅞ in. (4.75 cm) wide. Cross cut these strips into 126 1⅞-in. (4.75-cm) squares. Cross cut these squares on one diagonal to form 252 half-square triangles for the pieced blocks in Border 5.

- One strip, 6¾ in. (17 cm) wide. Cross cut this strip into four 6¾-in. (17-cm) squares. Cross cut these squares on one diagonal to form eight setting triangles for Border 5.

- Five strips 1½ in. (4 cm) wide for triangle blocks in Border 5.

From the blue binding fabric, cut:

- Nine strips, 3 in. (7.5 cm) wide

Cutting the appliqué shapes

To cut the appliqué shapes, place the template on the right side of the relevant fabric and trace around it using a silver gel pen. To cut the circles with Templates B, D, E, I, and J, trace onto the wrong side of the fabric to make the circles using the foil method (see page 133). Cut out the shapes, cutting ¼ in. (6 mm) from the gel-pen line using fabric scissors:

Template A: cut one heart from eggplant floral fabric. (Move the template around to fussy cut the heart if you wish.)

Template B: cut one circle from blue floral fabric and four from light blue floral for the corner flowers

Template C: cut one flower from pink floral fabric for the center flower and four from hot pink floral fabric for the corner flowers

Template D: cut one circle from solid (plain) eggplant fabric

Template E: fold a 10-in. (25-cm) square in four, place the template on the folded edge, and cut one circle from green floral fabric

Template F: cut six triangles from yellow fabric for the star

Template G: fold a 16-in. (40.5-cm) square in four, place the template on the folded edge, and cut one circle from solid (plain) eggplant fabric

Template H: cut four from blue floral fabric for the jagged border

Template I: cut 14 circles from 5-in. (12.5-cm) squares

Template J: cut 56 circles from 5-in. (12.5-cm) squares for appliqué blocks

Appliqué

There are a lot of small blocks to appliqué in this quilt. Due to their small size they make a great carry-around project for while you are piecing the blocks! Before beginning, prepare the circle pieces into perfect circles using the foil technique on page 133. Do not do this for Template G because it is too large—it will be needle turned like the other shapes (see page 129).

1 Center the eggplant floral Template A heart on the blue floral Template B circle. Lift the edges and place dots of glue on the back of the heart, not too close to the edge so that you can still turn the seam allowance under.

2 When the glue has dried (about 2 minutes), finger press around the edge of the heart, thread a straw needle with thread to match the fabric you are stitching, and knot the end. Appliqué the heart to the blue floral fabric, following the instructions for needle-turn appliqué on page 129. Refer to page 131 for details of how to stitch into V shapes and turn sharp points.

3 Turn the block over and carefully cut the fabric away from behind the heart, cutting ¼ in. (6 mm) in from the stitching line to reduce the bulk.

4 Center the blue floral circle on the pink floral Template C flower and repeat steps 2 and 3. Center the flower on the solid (plain) eggplant Template D circle, appliqué in place, then cut away. Center the circle on the green floral Template E circle, appliqué in place, then cut away.

5 Fold the gray-and-orange striped background square into quarters and finger press to leave a crease. Center the Template G solid (plain) eggplant circle on the gray-and-orange striped background square, appliqué in place, then cut away.

6 Center the built-up appliquéd circle on the Template G eggplant circle. Lift the edges of the appliquéd circle and put the bases of the Template F star points underneath, making sure that the top and bottom star points align with the vertical crease on the striped background square and the "V" formed by the two points on each side align with the horizontal crease.

7 When you are happy with the placement, glue and stitch the appliquéd circle and the star points in place, then cut away the excess fabric from behind the stitching.

8 Center a Template H blue floral piece on each 4½ x 17-in. (11.5 x 43-cm) piece of solid (plain) eggplant fabric. Glue, then appliqué in place, and cut away the excess fabric from behind. Following the instructions for preparing circles on page 133 and referring to the photo of the quilt on page 121, prepare the 14 Template I circles and glue and then appliqué them between the peaks of two of the borders. This is Border 1.

9 Center a prepared Template J circle on a 4½-in. (11.5-cm) eggplant square and appliqué in place. Repeat to make 56 appliquéd circle squares. Cut away the fabric from behind.

10 Center a prepared Template B light blue floral circle on a Template C hot pink flower and appliqué in place. Center the flower on an 8¾-in. (22.5-cm) eggplant square and stitch. Repeat to make four corner flowers in total.

Sewing

11 Sew all the blue 1⅞-in. (4.75-cm) half-square triangles to an eggplant half-square triangle to form squares. Press the seams toward the blue fabric and trim the ears. Sew another eggplant half-square triangle to each remaining side of the blue triangle (see Diagram 1). Make 84 of these sets.

12 Sew one of these sets to each side of a 2⅞-in. (7.25-cm) blue half-square triangle (see Diagrams 2 and 3). Set aside.

13 Sew a pink or yellow 1¾-in. (4.5-cm) strip to each side of an eggplant 1½-in. (4-cm) strip and press the seams toward the light fabrics. Make five sets like this.

14 Using Template K, cut triangles from the strips made in step 13, as shown in Diagram 4, making sure that the bottom (longest) edge of the triangle is always lined up with the outside edge of the fabric. You will have a bit of fabric at the top of the strip each time that is too big for the template, but that is alright. The triangles should be the same size as the template. Cut 56 triangles.

15 Sew a Template K triangle to the bottom of each of the 28 pieced blocks made in step 12 (see Diagram 5).

Assembly

Border 1

16 With the points facing inward, find the center of one of the Template H blue triangle border pieces without the dots from Step 8 and the center of the top of the center block, and pin the two right sides together. Pin the ends and pin in between, easing as you go if needed. Stitch. Repeat at the bottom of the block. Press the seams toward the borders.

17 Sew a 4½-in. (11.5-cm) eggplant square to each end of the two Border 1 pieces with the dots appliquéd onto them. Pin and stitch these pieces to the sides of the center block, as above.

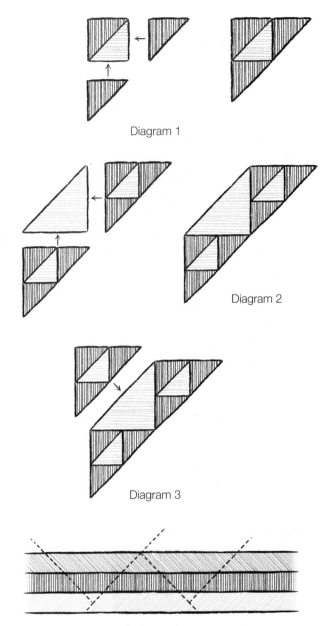

Diagram 1

Diagram 2

Diagram 3

Diagram 4

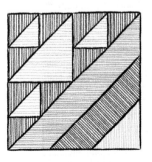

Diagram 5

Border 2

18 Measure the quilt through the center. It should measure 25 in. (63.5 cm). With right sides together, pin the center of a Border 2 strip to the center of the top of the quilt. Sew, beginning and ending the stitching ¼ in. (6 mm) from the edges of the quilt. Press toward the border. Add the other three Border 2 strips in the same way, beginning and ending all the stitching ¼ in. (6 mm) from the edges of the quilt. Using a rotary ruler, mark the top border and the side border at a 45-degree angle and trim ¼ in. (6 mm) beyond the marked line. Stitch the top and side borders together along the marked line and press the seam towards the side border. Repeat with all four corners.

Border 3

19 Sew seven appliquéd circle squares from step 9 together in a row. Make four rows. Sew a solid (plain) eggplant 4½-in. (11.5-cm) square to each end of two of the rows.

20 Sew a row of seven appliquéd circle squares to the top edge of the quilt and press toward Border 2. Repeat at the bottom edge of the quilt, and then add the border strips with the solid (plain) eggplant squares to the sides of the quilt.

Border 4

21 Sew a light blue strip to all four edges of the quilt top and miter the corners, as in step 18. Press toward Border 4.

Border 5

22 Referring to Diagram 6, sew 24 of the appliquéd circle blocks from step 9 and the 28 pieced blocks from steps 11–15 together in diagonal strips, adding red setting triangles as shown. Join the diagonal strips together into rows, beginning with an eggplant triangle and a pieced triangle and refering to the photo of the quilt on page 121 for placement. Sew four rows with six circles and seven pieced blocks each.

23 Pin and sew one Border 5 to the top and bottom of the quilt and press toward Border 4. Sew an 8¾-in. (22.5-cm) appliquéd flower square from step 10 to each end of the remaining two Border 5 strips, then sew these strips to the sides of the quilt in the same way.

Border 6

24 Measure the quilt top through the center in both directions: it should measure 59½ in. (151 cm). Remove the selvages (selvedges) and sew all the green floral strips together in one long strip. Cut four 63-in. (160-cm) lengths. Sew to all four edges of the quilt top and miter the corners, as in step 18. Press toward Border 6.

Diagram 6

Border 7

25 Measure the quilt top through the center in both directions: it should measure 62½ in. (159 cm). Remove the selvages (selvedges) and sew all the 4½-in. (11.5-cm) strips of multi-colored floral fabric together in one long strip. Cut four 62½-in. (140-cm) lengths. Find the center of the top of the quilt and the center of one border strip, and pin the two right sides together. Pin the ends, then pin in between, and stitch. Attach the bottom border in the same way.

26 Sew an appliquéd circle block from step 9 to each end of the last two Border 7 strips. Pin and sew to the sides of the quilt. Your quilt top is complete.

Backing, quilting, and binding

27 Cut the backing fabric crosswise into two pieces, each 78 in. (200 cm) long. Remove the selvages (selvedges) and stitch the pieces together along one long edge. Press the seam open and press the backing piece carefully.

28 If hand quilting, tape the backing fabric right side down to the floor or a very large table using masking tape, smoothing out any creases as you go. Lay the batting (wadding) on the backing fabric, with the quilt top right side up on top. Smooth any creases and hand baste (tack) the three layers together, using large stitches and working from the center out. The backing and batting (wadding) should be larger than the top for ease of quilting; don't be tempted to trim them back.

29 Quilt as desired and bind the quilt, following the instructions on pages 136–139.

Note on quilting

Lady Marmalade was custom machine quilted by Kim Bradley.

techniques

sewing techniques

Here is some information for you about some of the techniques used in this book. Some of the techniques are things you may never have tried before, and some of them are things that I might attack a little differently than you are used to. Make sure you read the instructions through carefully before starting your quilt.

Partial seams

There are times when a quilt cannot be put together in straight lines. Due to the step-downs or corner meeting places in the pattern, it cannot be sewn together in rows. The partial seam technique is used in *All That and the Hatter* (see page 110).

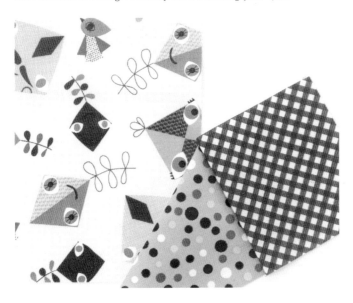

1 To close the partial seam, first sew the red square to the green square along its length.

2 Then close the seam along the length of the rectangle, as shown.

Working partial seams

The partial seam technique is very important for piecing All That and the Hatter, and it can be confusing. If you are finding it difficult, I have a video class on this technique at www.craftsy.com, or you can try making the Step Down dolly quilt from my book *Quilting: from little things* first to get the technique right before you start on a larger quilt.

Foundation piecing

Foundation piecing is a clever technique used to make blocks of exactly the same size, to achieve accurate designs with sharp points, or to stabilize scraps and control bias stretching. It involves, as the name implies, the use of paper or fabric as a base, or foundation, for piecing. Lines drawn on the underside of the foundation allow straight accurate seams that make it possible to sew even the most advanced blocks perfectly.

Foundation papers can be purchased in quilt or craft shops. The block designs need to be traced or copied onto the papers, so you will need at least one page per block. Be sure to choose a paper that feeds into your printer or photocopier. In some cases, it is possible to use standard copier paper. If seams intersect, however, this is not such a good option. The paper is removed once the blocks are sewn and this task can be tedious if the paper cannot be removed easily.

To foundation piece a crazy block as mentioned in Slash That Stash on page 79, begin crazy piecing in the center of the foundation and sew through all layers making sure the fabric is kept flat for each seam. Build the block outward until it is slightly larger than the foundation piece and then trim.

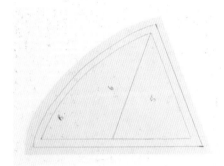 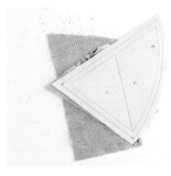 

1 The first step is to trace or copy the pattern for the desired number of blocks onto the foundation paper. Set your sewing machine to a small stitch—say 1.5—which helps when the time comes to remove the papers later. Sewing through the paper will dull your needle, so remember to change to a fresh needle when doing other sewing.

2 Place the fabrics right sides together, with the paper right side up on top, as shown. Hold the paper up to a light to be sure that the fabric covers the necessary area. Be aware of where the fabric will be sewn and make sure that it will cover the next seam line when pressed flat. Sew the line, trim off the excess seam allowance, then flip the strip and press it in place. Be sure to leave a ¼-in. (6-mm) seam allowance on the last strip.

3 When the block is completely stitched, fold over the first strip at the seam and finger press along the sewing line. Use a seam ripper to gently help loosen the paper before pulling it away. Do not rip out the paper or the stitches will loosen.

appliqué

There are various appliqué techniques, but my favorite is the needle-turn method, described below. Whatever method you choose, complete all the appliqué before you piece the blocks together, unless otherwise instructed.

All the quilts in this book are suited to machine appliqué. If you wish to machine appliqué your quilts, remove the seam allowance from around each shape before you cut it out.

Before beginning the appliqué, decide where you want your shapes to sit on the background block. Use a sharp 2B pencil or other marker to lightly trace the shapes onto the background fabric. A light box is useful when tracing; if you don't have one, tape the design to be traced onto a sunny window, lightly tape the fabric over it, then trace the design.

Remember that some designs need to have their elements sewn down in a particular order. For example, when sewing a flower, the stem needs to be sewn first so that it sits under the flower petals, then the petals added, and lastly the flower center and the leaves. If you are working on a complicated appliqué design and you think you might get confused, draw or photocopy a diagram of the complete design, determine the order in which the pieces need to be laid down, and then number the shapes on the diagram so that you can keep track.

Needle-turn appliqué

1 Using a sharp 2B pencil, trace the template shapes onto template plastic or cardstock. Using paper scissors (not your fabric scissors), cut out along the traced line.

2 Place the template on the right side of the fabric and trace around it, taking care to leave space between the pieces for a seam allowance. I use a silver gel pen for marking my sewing lines, first, because it's reflective and shows up on any fabric, and second, because it's really easy to see whether or not you have turned your shape under neatly or not. If you can still see silver, you haven't got the shape right! However, gel pen does not wash off. Once you have traced your shape onto the fabric, you're married to it, so be careful with that tracing!

3 Cut the shapes out a scant ¼ in. (6 mm) from the gel line. Finger press along the line all around the shape, including into any curves or points. Do not be tempted to iron the seam in: a finger-pressed line is easy to manipulate, whereas an ironed line is difficult to change if you iron a point into a crease or a line in the wrong spot. You will also be very likely to burn your fingers! Finger pressing is a guide to help you turn the fabric as you sew.

4 Position the pieces on the background block, using the traced outline or photograph supplied with the pattern as a guide. Note which parts of the pieces may go under others; dotted lines on the templates indicate which parts of each piece should be placed under adjacent pieces.

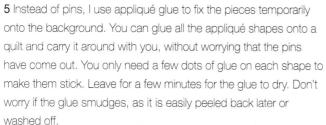

5 Instead of pins, I use appliqué glue to fix the pieces temporarily onto the background. You can glue all the appliqué shapes onto a quilt and carry it around with you, without worrying that the pins have come out. You only need a few dots of glue on each shape to make them stick. Leave for a few minutes for the glue to dry. Don't worry if the glue smudges, as it is easily peeled back later or washed off.

6 Thread your appliqué needle with thread to match the appliqué fabric. You should always match your appliqué thread to the color of the fabric shape that you are appliquéing, not to the background. I use very long, fine straw needles for appliqué: the finer the needle, the smaller you can make your stitches for invisible appliqué. You can start anywhere, but try to never start on an inside curve.

7 Tie a knot in the thread and come up from the back to the front of the background fabric, catching the very edge of the appliqué shape with your needle, as shown.

Points and curves

The best way to get a sharp point is this: sew all the way up to the point on one side. Fold the fabric down 90 degrees under the point, then sweep the remaining fabric downward and underneath the main part of the point.

Take a stitch right at the point again and give it a sharp tug, then continue sewing down the other side of the point.

When you get to an inside curve, you've reached your next challenge! You can sew all around the outside curves without clipping, but inside curves need clipping. Using very sharp, small scissors, carefully clip up to the silver line, about ¼ in. (6 mm) apart, all around the inner curve.

I never clip anything until I am ready to sew it. If you do, it can fray and get messy. Sew all the way up to the curve before you clip, and then sew the curve right away.

8 Go down into the background fabric right next to where you came up, run your needle along underneath the background, and come up again right on the edge of the appliqué shape, as shown. Don't try to turn the whole edge under before you sew it; just turn under the small section you are working on. This makes it easier to keep track of the gel pen line and make sure that you turn it all under.

9 Sew all around the cut edge of the appliqué shape in this manner. Your stitches should just catch the edge of the fabric and be quite small and close together, which will make the appliqué strong and avoid it being torn or looking puckered. Continue until you have sewn all around the outside of the shape and then tie the thread off at the back with a small knot.

10 Turn the block over and make a small cut at the back of the shape, taking care not to cut the appliqué. Cut away the background fabric underneath the appliqué. Be sure not to cut closer than ¼ in. (6 mm) away from the seam lines. Although it is not necessary, removing the fabric in this way makes the appliqué sit nicely and creates fewer layers to quilt through, especially where appliqué pieces overlap. Repeat this process with each shape. Remove the background from under each piece before you apply the next one.

Making a quick bias strip

Bias strips are used in appliqué for making vines or stems for flowers, basket handles, and the like. The strips need to be cut on the bias so that they can be easily ironed and glued into a curve without puckering. A fat quarter is useful for making bias strips for small projects, as they are square and you will get a good length of strip from one square.

1 Take the piece of fabric you want to make into bias and make a 45-degree cut along one corner, using the 45-degree angle line on your patchwork ruler. Using this angle, cut strips from the fabric that are ½ in. (12 mm) wider than you want the finished bias strip to be.

2 To join strips together, place them right sides together at right angles to each other and sew on the diagonal until they are as long as you require. Fold back, trim the seam allowances, and press the seams open to reduce bulk when stitching.

3 Using a Hera marker, score a line ¼ in. (6 mm) in from the edge on both sides of the strip and all the way along the length, as shown.

4 Iron the edges of the bias strip under on both sides along the score marks to make bias tape.

Applying bias curves

1 First, mark the line of the bias curve that you want to appliqué lightly on the background fabric with a pencil. Take your bias strips and the background appliqué fabric to the ironing board.

2 Put the beginning of your bias strip on the beginning of the pencil line and put the tip of the iron onto the bias. Pull the bias strip out in front of the iron and slowly begin pressing the strip along the pencil line you made to press the curve in.

3 If you have a strip longer than the ironing board, iron as far as you can go along the curve and stop. Lift the bias strip up carefully and put dots of glue along the pencil line, then replace the strip and let dry. Shift the background fabric along the ironing board and repeat until you have glued the bias to the background.

Perfect appliqué circles

Turning a perfect circle can be difficult with hand appliqué. An easy method for turning the circles is to use a cardstock or Mylar template and aluminum foil.

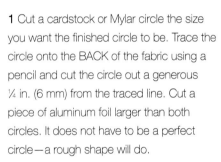

1 Cut a cardstock or Mylar circle the size you want the finished circle to be. Trace the circle onto the BACK of the fabric using a pencil and cut the circle out a generous ¼ in. (6 mm) from the traced line. Cut a piece of aluminum foil larger than both circles. It does not have to be a perfect circle—a rough shape will do.

2 Place the foil shiny side down on the ironing board first, then the fabric circle right side down, then the cardstock or Mylar circle on top, aligning with the circle you traced. Pull all the edges of the foil up to cover the cardstock circle, pulling the edges in as you do so and smoothing the curve so that you don't have any pointy edges anywhere.

3 Turn the foil circle over to the shiny side and press with the iron. Give the foil a few seconds to cool down, then open the foil up and remove the fabric and the cardstock or Mylar. You now have a perfect circle ready to glue and appliqué to your background fabric.

constructing your quilt

If a layout diagram is given, be sure to refer to it as well as to the photograph. Many quilt designs, especially complex ones using more than one type of block, feature optical illusions caused by the way in which the various components are combined.

Sometimes the logic of the quilt's construction will not become clear until you look at a layout diagram.

Adding borders

Borders may be added for decorative effect or to increase the quilt's size, or both. They may have squared-off or mitered corners. The quilt pattern will tell you what length to cut the borders, but you should always measure your quilt before cutting the border fabric, and then adjust the length of the border strips if necessary.

Measure in both directions through the middle of the quilt rather than along the edges. This is because the edges may have distorted a little during the making of the quilt, especially if any of the edge pieces are bias cut. Use these measurements to calculate the length of each border.

Squared-off borders

If you are adding squared-off borders, the side borders will be the length of the quilt top. The top and bottom borders will be the width of the quilt top with the side borders added. Unless a pattern indicates otherwise, sew the side borders on first, press the seams toward the border, then add the top and bottom borders.

Mitered borders

If you are adding borders with mitered corners, each border will need to be the width or length of the quilt, plus twice the width of the border, to allow enough fabric for mitering, plus seam allowance. Sew each border to the edge of the quilt, beginning and ending the seam a precise ¼ in. (6 mm) from the edge of the quilt. Fold the quilt so that the side and the top are flush and the two

border strips extend to the side. Use your ruler and a 45-degree-angle line to mark a line from the ¼-in. (6-mm) point to the edge of the strip.

Sew along this line and check before cutting: it must lie flat. When confident, trim off the extra and repeat for all four corners.

Layering the quilt

Once you have added all the borders, and before you can begin quilting, you need to assemble all three layers of the quilt.

The batting (wadding) and backing fabric should both be at least 4 in. (10 cm) larger all around than the quilt top. You may need to join two widths of fabric, or add a strip of scraps or leftover blocks, to obtain a large enough piece for the backing. Press any seams in the backing open to reduce bulk when quilting. If you need to join two pieces of batting, butt them up together without overlapping and machine-zigzag a seam.

Press the quilt top and backing fabric. Lay the backing fabric right side down on a large, flat, clean surface (preferably one that is not carpeted), smooth it out carefully, then tape it to the surface using masking tape. Tape it at intervals along all sides, but do not tape the corners, as this will cause the bias to stretch out of shape.

Place the batting (wadding) on top of the backing fabric and smooth it out. Center the well-pressed quilt top, right side up, on top of the batting (wadding), ensuring that the top and backing are square to each other. Smooth out.

Tape the backing right side down, then layer the wadding (batting) and the quilt top on top. The wadding (batting) should be larger than the quilt top and the backing should be larger again.

Types of batting (wadding)

Some battings (waddings) need to be quilted closer together than others to stop them from drifting around within the quilt or fragmenting when washed. Polyester batting requires less quilting than cotton or wool batting. However, some polyester battings have a tendency to fight the sewing machine.

Wool battings (usually actually a wool/polyester or a wool/ cotton blend) provide more warmth and comfort than polyester battings. However, they require more quilting, and those that are not needle-punched tend to pill. Needle-punched wool blends are more stable and require less quilting. Traditional cotton battings require a lot of quilting, as much as every ½–3 in. (12–75 mm). Needle-punched cotton battings are more stable and can be quilted up to 10 in. (25 cm) apart. Ask your quilt store for advice if you are unsure of what to choose.

Basting (tacking)

Once you have assembled the three layers, you need to baste (tack) them together ready for quilting. Basting can be done with safety pins or long hand stitches.

If you are using safety pins, start from the center of the quilt and pin through all three layers at intervals of about 8 in. (20 cm). If you are intending to machine quilt, make sure the pins are kept away from the lines to be quilted. Once the whole quilt is safety-pinned, it can be moved.

If you are intending to hand quilt, baste the whole quilt both horizontally and vertically, always working from the center out, using long hand stitches at intervals of about 6 in. (15 cm). Using a curved needle is a good idea, as this makes the task easier on the wrists.

Do not baste using hand stitches if you intend to machine-quilt, as the basting threads will get caught under the presser foot. Do not use safety pins if you are hand quilting, as the pins prevent the hoop from sitting evenly.

Some quilting stores offer a machine-basting service. This can be a worthwhile investment, especially if you are going to be doing fine hand quilting in the traditional manner, a task that can take months or even years.

Remove the basting stitches or safety pins only once all the quilting is complete.

quilting

Quilting can be fairly rudimentary, its main purpose being to hold together the layers of the quilt, or it can be decorative and sometimes extremely elaborate. Machine quilting is quick, but nothing beats hand quilting for sheer heirloom beauty and a soft hand to the finished quilt.

Designs for hand quilting, or elaborate designs for machine quilting, are generally marked on the quilt top before the quilt's layers are sandwiched together. On pale fabrics, the marking is done lightly in pencil; on dark fabrics, use a special quilter's silver pencil. Pencil lines can be erased later.

If you intend to quilt straight lines or a cross-hatched design, masking tape can be used to mark out the lines on the quilt top. Such tape comes in various widths, from ¼ in. (6 mm) upward. Free-flowing lines can be drawn on with a chalk pencil.

If you intend to outline-quilt by machine, you may be able to sew straight enough lines by eye; if not, you will need to mark the quilt top first.

Hand quilting

Quilting by hand produces a softer line than machine quilting and will give a hand-loved quality to quilts. Most of the quilts in this book are quilted using perle cotton, since it is often easier for beginners to work with and stands out vividly against the fabric's surface, although traditional waxed quilting thread can be used if you prefer.

To quilt by hand, the fabric needs to be held in a frame (also known as a quilting hoop). Free-standing frames are available, but hand-held ones are cheaper, more portable, and just as effective. One edge of a hand-held frame can be rested against a table or bench to enable you to keep both hands free.

Hand quilting, like machine quilting, should commence in the center of the quilt and proceed outward. To commence hand quilting, place the plain (inner) ring of the frame under the center of the quilt. Position the other ring, with the screw, over the top of the quilt to align with the inner ring. Tighten the screw so that the fabric in the frame becomes firm, but not drum-tight.

For traditional quilting, choose the smallest needle that you feel comfortable with. (These needles are known as "betweens.") For quilting with perle cotton, use a good-quality crewel embroidery needle (I use a No 9).

1 Thread the needle with about 18 in. (45 cm) of thread. Knot the end of the thread with a one-loop knot and take the needle down through the quilt top into the batting (wadding), a short distance from where you want to start quilting. Tug the thread slightly so that the knot pulls through the fabric into the batting, making the starting point invisible.

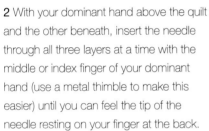

2 With your dominant hand above the quilt and the other beneath, insert the needle through all three layers at a time with the middle or index finger of your dominant hand (use a metal thimble to make this easier) until you can feel the tip of the needle resting on your finger at the back.

3 Without pushing the needle through, rock the needle back to the top of the quilt and use your underneath finger to push the tip of the needle up. Put your upper thumb down in front of the needle tip while pushing up from the back, as shown. This will make a small "hill" in the fabric.

4 Push the needle through the fabric. This makes one stitch. To take several stitches at once, push the needle along to the required stitch length, then dip the tip into the fabric and repeat the above technique. Gently pull the stitches to indent the stitch line evenly. You should always quilt toward yourself, as this reduces hand and shoulder strain, so turn the quilt in the required direction. You can protect your underneath finger using a stick-on plastic shield such as a Thimble-It. You can also use a leather thimble, although this does make it more difficult to feel how far the needle has come through, and thus more difficult to keep your stitches neat and even.

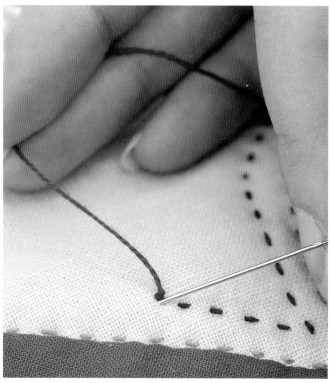

Finishing a thread

1 Hold the thread out to the side with your left hand, and loop a one-loop knot using the needle.

2 Slide the loose knot down the thread until it lies directly on the quilt top, and tighten the knot. Take the needle back down through the hole the thread is coming out of and slide it away through the batting (wadding), as shown. Bring the needle back up to the top of the quilt and give the thread a tug. The knot will follow down into the hole and lodge in the batting. Cut the thread close to the surface.

Machine quilting

You may want to machine quilt your quilt yourself, but I use and recommend a professional quilting service for a couple of good reasons.

First, finished quilts are usually quite large and, consequently, rather cumbersome. It really is a fairly tricky job to manipulate the bulk of the quilt on a domestic sewing machine, even using a specialized walking foot. Having pieced your precious quilt so carefully, it would be a shame to spoil it now with puckers and distortions.

Second, professional machine quilters offer a large range of quilting patterns to suit every need and taste and can also advise you on a design that will enhance all your careful work.

If you want to learn to machine quilt, I recommend taking a class at your local quilt shop or online.

binding

The binding is the narrow strip of folded fabric that wraps around the outer edges of the quilt to hide the raw edges of top, batting (wadding), and backing. There are many different methods of binding a quilt, but the technique detailed here is how I bind my quilts.

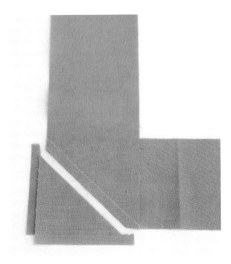

2 To seam the strips into a continuous length, fold under one end of one strip at a 45-degree angle and finger press a crease. Unfold. The crease line will become the seam line. Mark this line lightly with a pencil. With right sides together and the two fabric pieces at 90 degrees, align the angled cut end with the next strip of binding fabric. Align the ¼-in. (6-mm) measurement on a quilter's ruler with this line and trim off the corner. Sew the two strips together along the marked line. Press all seams to one side and trim off the ears, as shown.

1 From the width of the binding fabric, cut enough strips to equal the outside edge of your quilt, plus about 6 in. (15 cm) to allow for mitered corners and for the ends to be folded under. I cut my binding strips 3 in. (7.5 cm) wide and use a ½-in. (12-mm) seam when attaching them to the quilt.

3 Press the entire strip in half along its length, as shown. Doubling the fabric like this makes the binding more durable.

4 Trim the backing and the batting so that they are even with the edge of the quilt top. Beginning at one end of the binding strip, pin the binding to one edge of the quilt, starting about 4 in. (10 cm) in from a corner and aligning the raw edges. Attach a walking foot to your machine and machine sew the binding in place through all the layers of the quilt, using a ¼-in. (6-mm) seam allowance and mitering the corners.

Mitering corners

To miter corners, end the seam ¼ in. (6 mm) from the corner and fasten off. Fold the binding fabric up at a 45-degree angle, then fold it down so that the fold is level with the edge of the binding you have just sewn. Begin the next seam at the edge of the quilt and proceed as before. Repeat this process to miter all the corners.

When you approach the point at which the binding started, trim the excess, tuck the end of the binding under itself using a diagonal fold, and then stitch the rest of the seam.

Press the binding away from the quilt. Turn the binding to the back of the quilt and blind hem-stitch in place by hand to finish.

Your quilt is now complete!

Adding a label

Once you have finished your quilt, you should add a label so that future generations know who made it—especially if the quilt is a gift. There are pre-printed fabric labels that you can buy; alternatively, simply write on a nice piece of co-ordinating fabric with a laundry marker, and slipstitch it to the back of the quilt.

templates

Where instructions are given to add a seam allowance, you should add it to the fabric as you cut it out, not to the template.

all that and the hatter

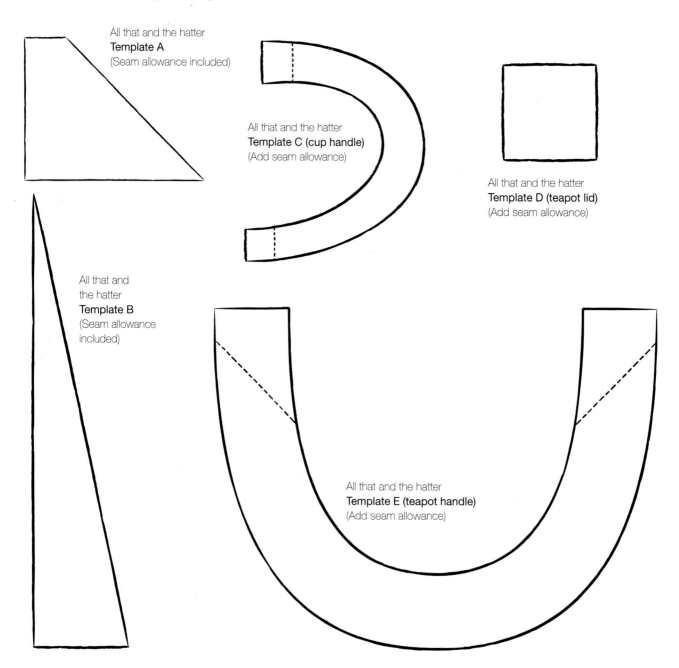

All that and the hatter
Template A
(Seam allowance included)

All that and the hatter
Template C (cup handle)
(Add seam allowance)

All that and the hatter
Template D (teapot lid)
(Add seam allowance)

All that and
the hatter
Template B
(Seam allowance
included)

All that and the hatter
Template E (teapot handle)
(Add seam allowance)

i love all the colors

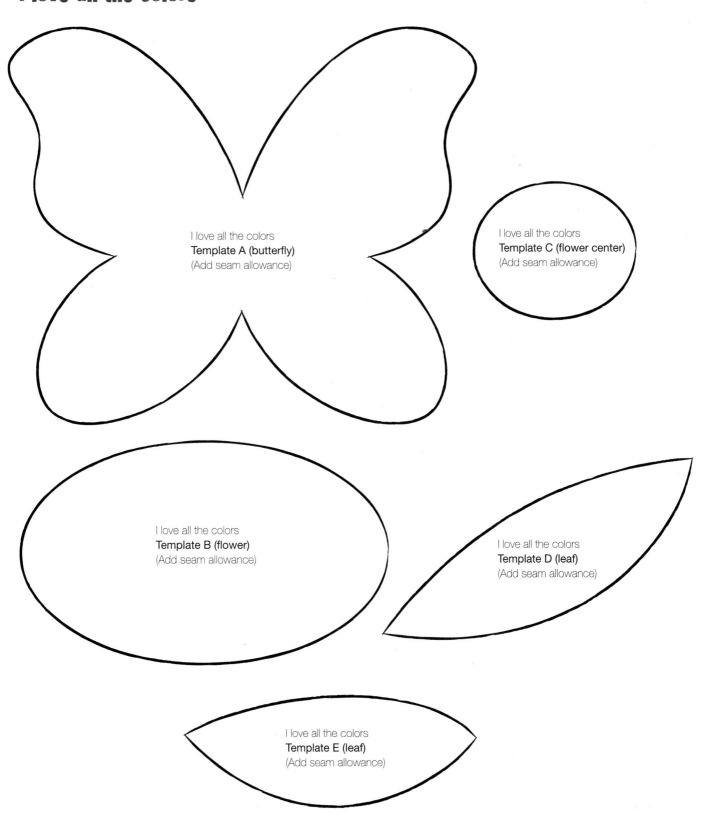

I love all the colors
Template A (butterfly)
(Add seam allowance)

I love all the colors
Template C (flower center)
(Add seam allowance)

I love all the colors
Template B (flower)
(Add seam allowance)

I love all the colors
Template D (leaf)
(Add seam allowance)

I love all the colors
Template E (leaf)
(Add seam allowance)

string-sane

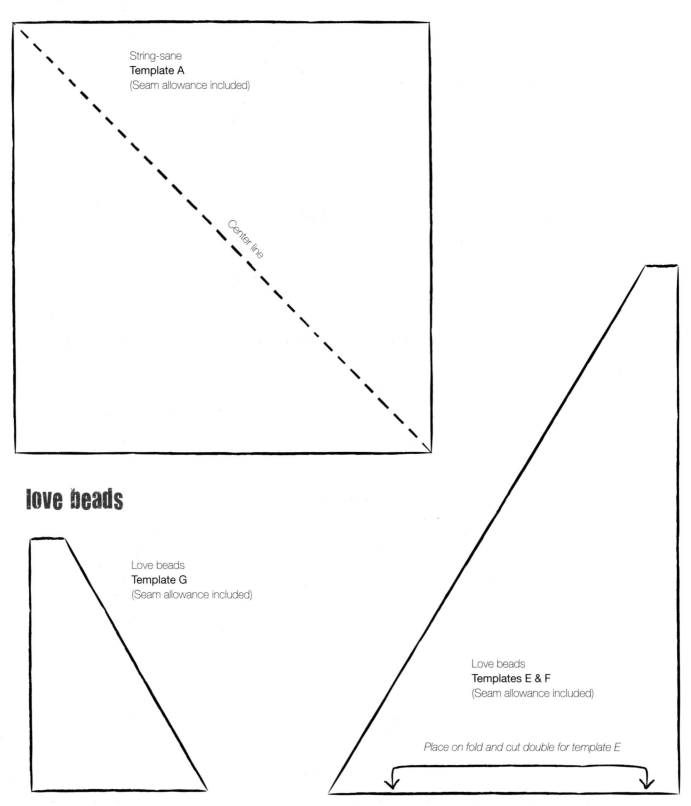

String-sane
Template A
(Seam allowance included)

Center line

love beads

Love beads
Template G
(Seam allowance included)

Love beads
Templates E & F
(Seam allowance included)

Place on fold and cut double for template E

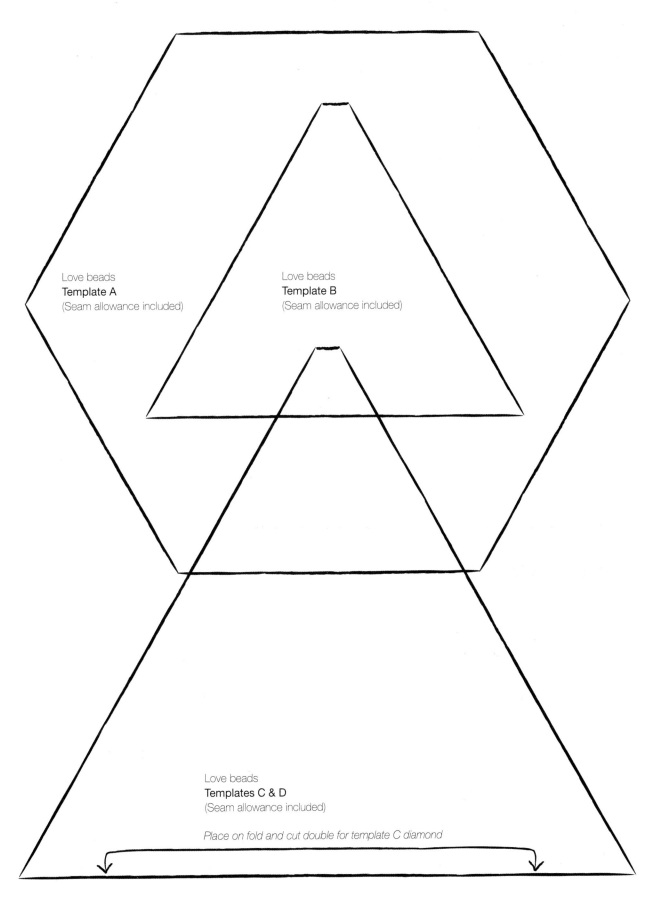

Love beads
Template A
(Seam allowance included)

Love beads
Template B
(Seam allowance included)

Love beads
Templates C & D
(Seam allowance included)

Place on fold and cut double for template C diamond

millefiori

Millefiori
Template A
(Add seam allowance)

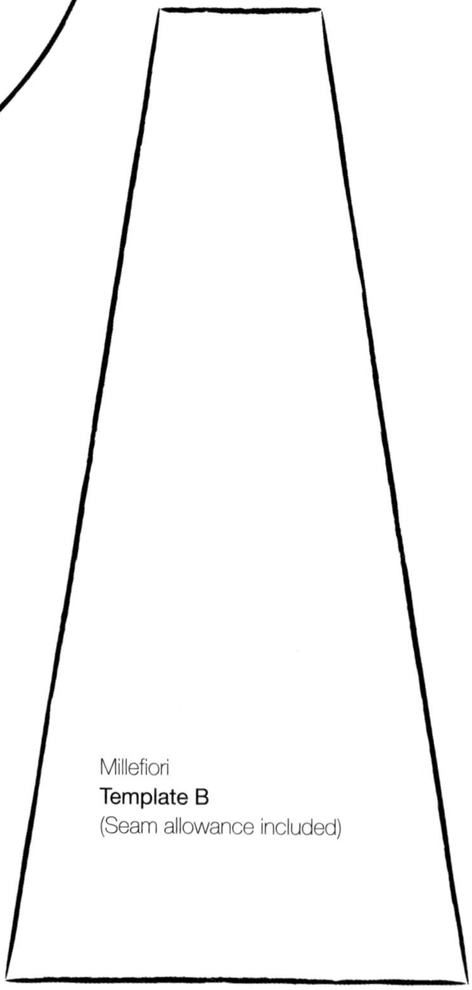

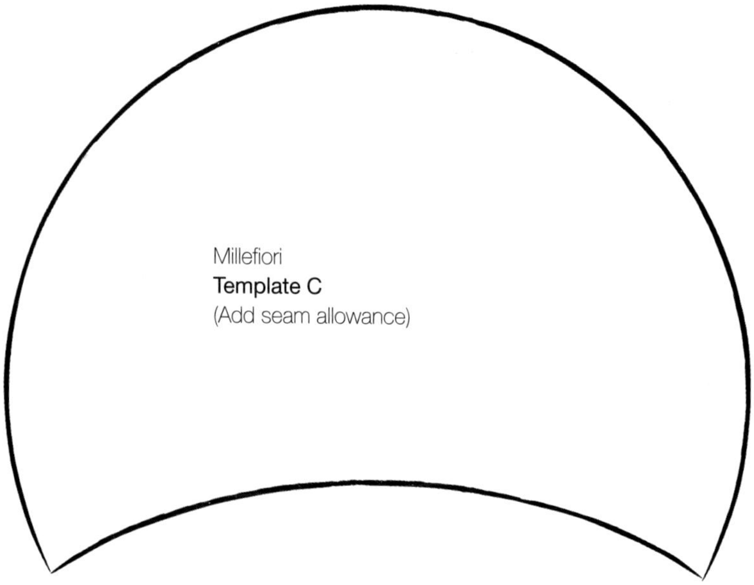

Millefiori
Template C
(Add seam allowance)

Millefiori
Template B
(Seam allowance included)

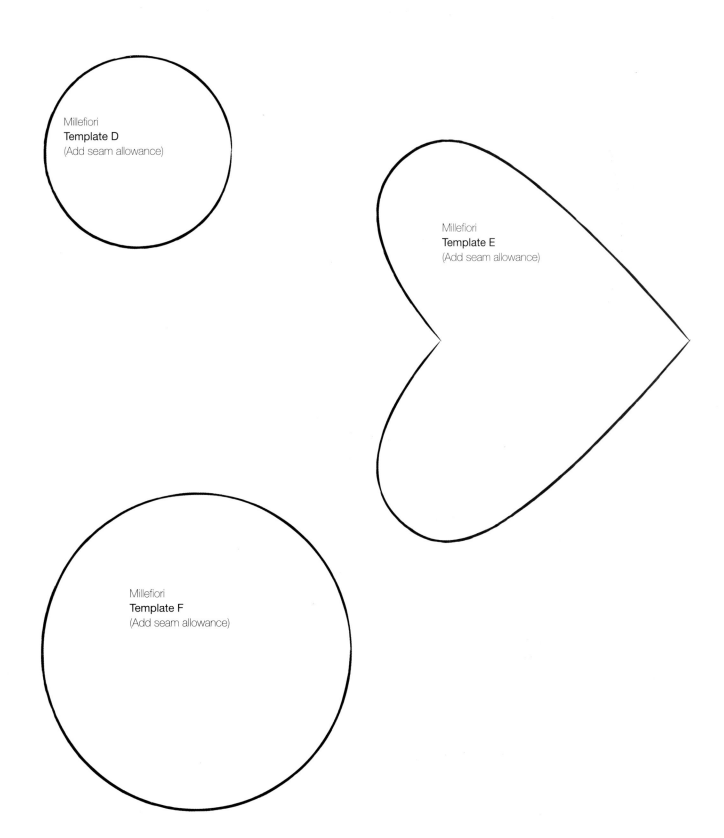

Millefiori
Template D
(Add seam allowance)

Millefiori
Template E
(Add seam allowance)

Millefiori
Template F
(Add seam allowance)

fancy that

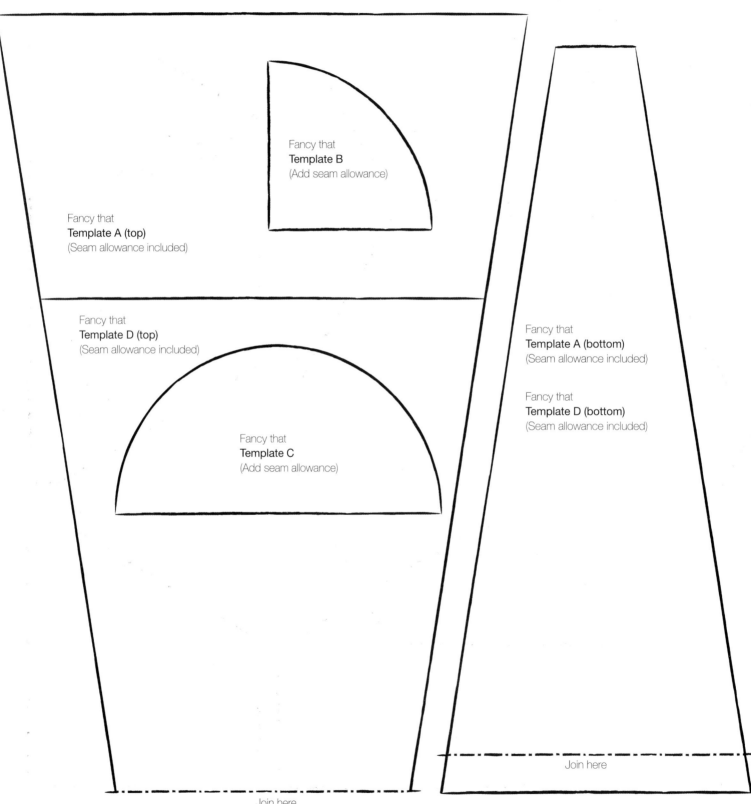

Fancy that
Template B
(Add seam allowance)

Fancy that
Template A (top)
(Seam allowance included)

Fancy that
Template D (top)
(Seam allowance included)

Fancy that
Template C
(Add seam allowance)

Fancy that
Template A (bottom)
(Seam allowance included)

Fancy that
Template D (bottom)
(Seam allowance included)

Join here

Join here

bangles

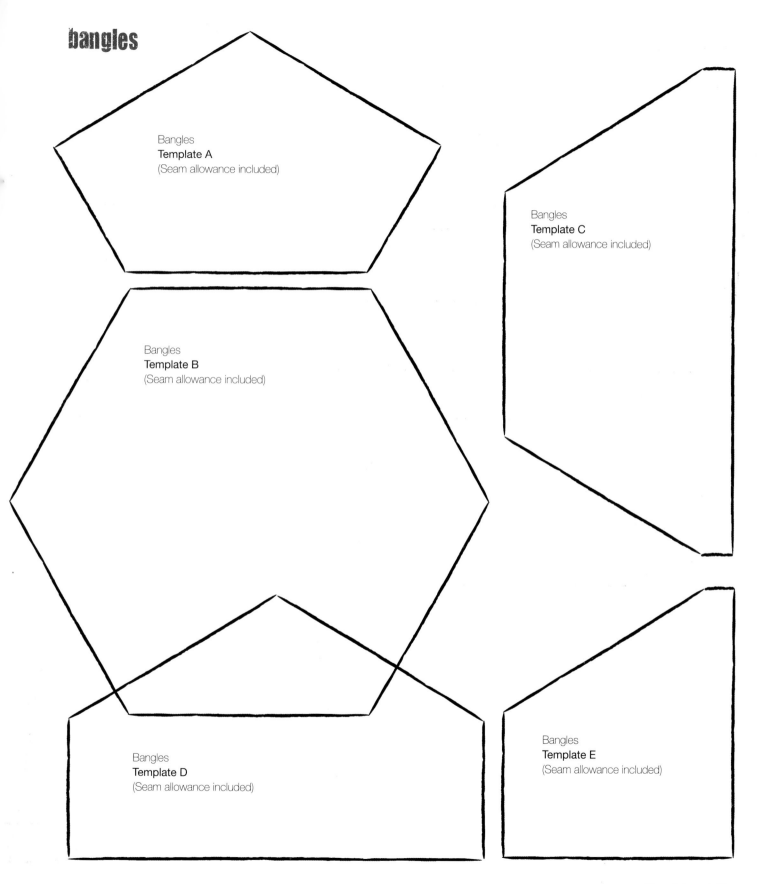

Bangles
Template A
(Seam allowance included)

Bangles
Template C
(Seam allowance included)

Bangles
Template B
(Seam allowance included)

Bangles
Template D
(Seam allowance included)

Bangles
Template E
(Seam allowance included)

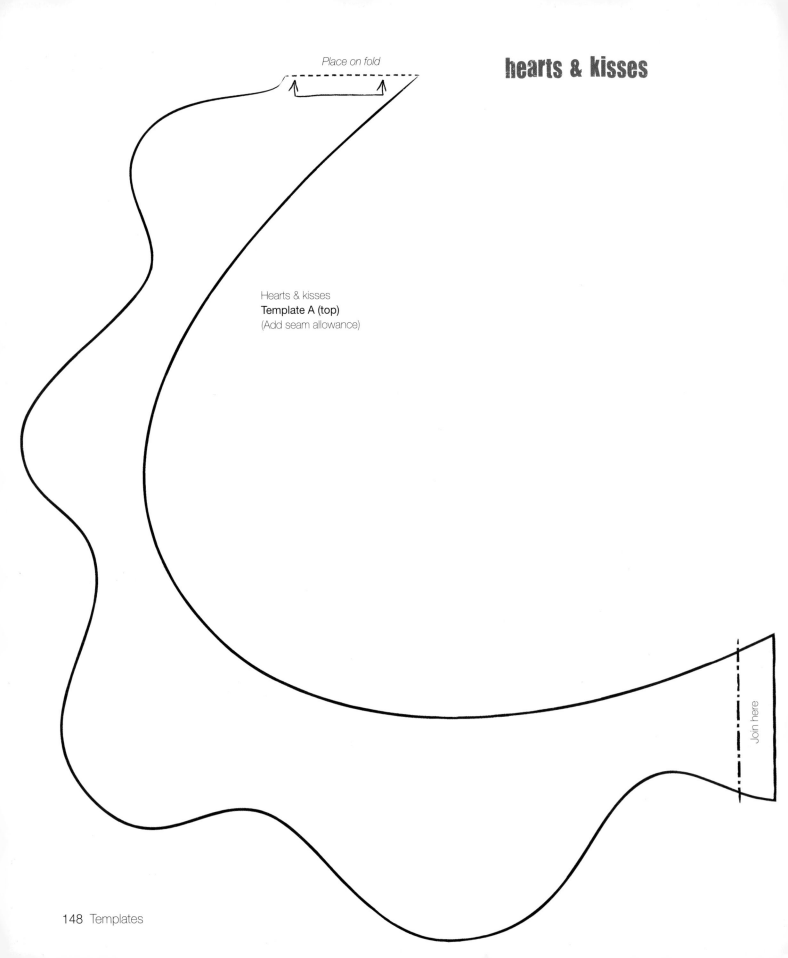

Place on fold

hearts & kisses

Hearts & kisses
Template A (top)
(Add seam allowance)

Join here

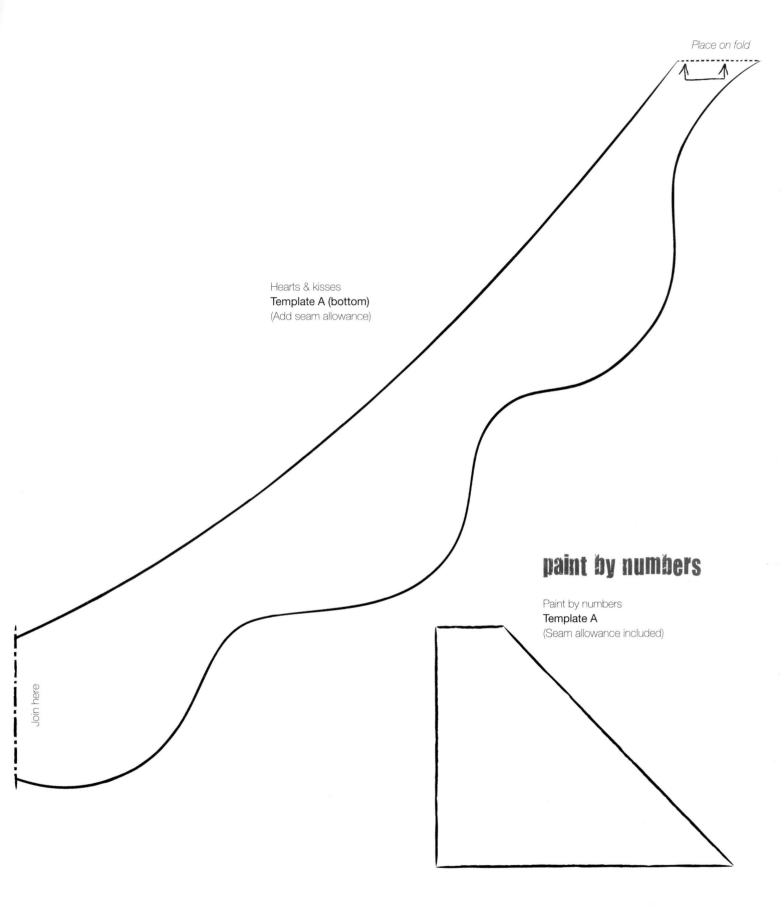

Hearts & kisses
Template A (bottom)
(Add seam allowance)

Join here

paint by numbers

Paint by numbers
Template A
(Seam allowance included)

lady marmalade

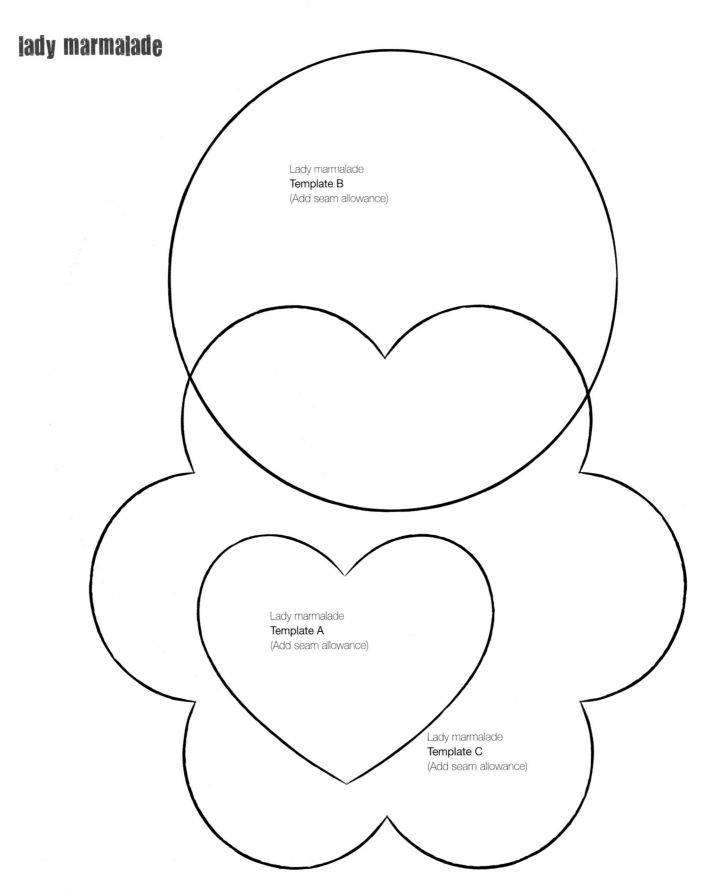

Lady marmalade
Template B
(Add seam allowance)

Lady marmalade
Template A
(Add seam allowance)

Lady marmalade
Template C
(Add seam allowance)

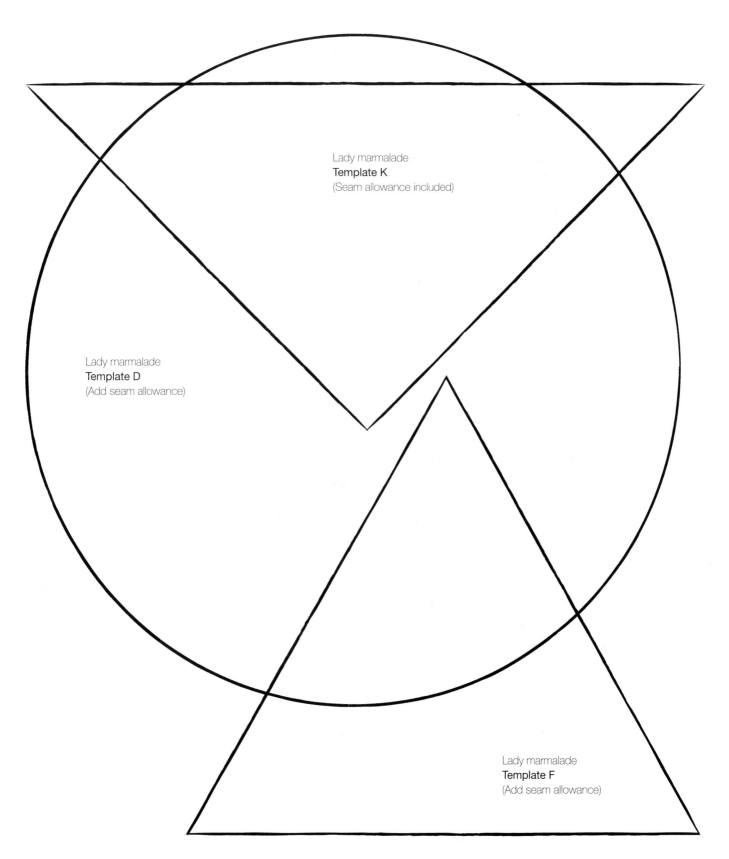

Lady marmalade
Template K
(Seam allowance included)

Lady marmalade
Template D
(Add seam allowance)

Lady marmalade
Template F
(Add seam allowance)

Lady marmalade
Template H (top)
(Seam allowance included)

Lady marmalade
Template H (bottom)
(Seam allowance included)

Join here

Join here

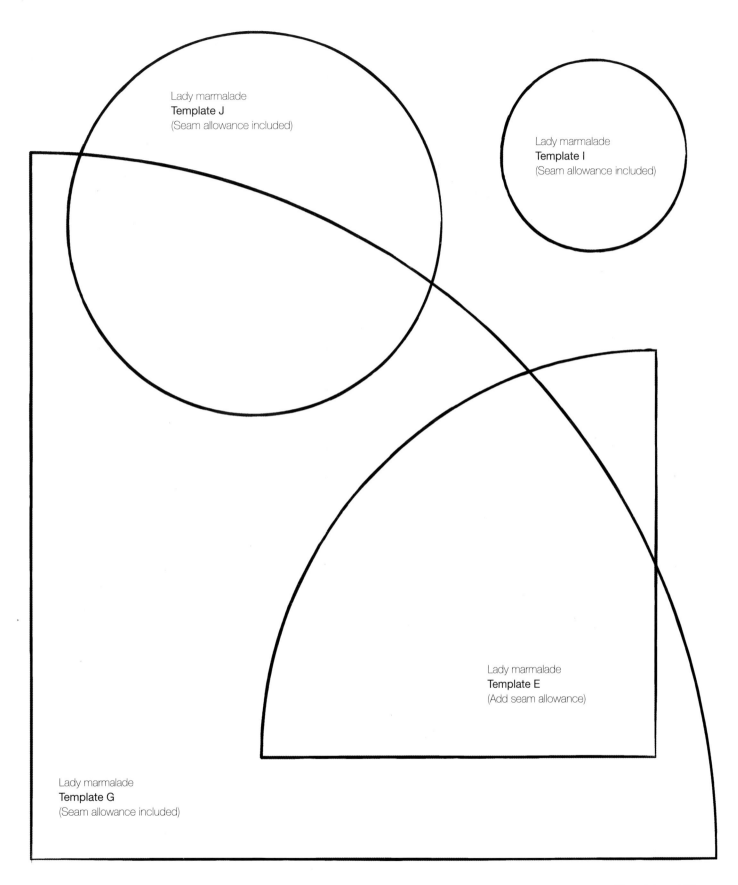

Lady marmalade
Template J
(Seam allowance included)

Lady marmalade
Template I
(Seam allowance included)

Lady marmalade
Template E
(Add seam allowance)

Lady marmalade
Template G
(Seam allowance included)

glossary

Appliqué
A technique in which small pieces of fabric are stitched to a background fabric.

Backing
The undermost layer of a quilt.

Basting (tacking)
A method of holding together several layers of fabric during quilting, so that they do not move around. Basting may be done using a long hand stitch, or with safety pins. The stitches or pins are removed once the quilting is complete.

Batting (wadding)
The middle layer of a quilt; also known as wadding.

Bias
The diagonal of a woven fabric, at a 45-degree angle to the straight grain (the warp and weft). Fabric cut on the bias stretches, so care must be taken when handling and sewing bias-cut pieces. Compare with grain.

Binding
The narrow strips of fabric (usually made of a double thickness) that enclose the raw edges and batting of a quilt.

Block
The basic unit of a patchwork quilt top. Blocks are usually square, but may be rectangular, hexagonal or other shapes. They may be plain (of one fabric only), appliquéd, or pieced.

Border
A strip of fabric (plain, appliquéd, or pieced) joined to the central panel of a quilt and used to frame it and also to add extra size.

Chain-piecing
A method of joining fabric pieces by machine in an assembly-line fashion, which speeds up the process and uses less thread. Pairs or sets of block pieces are fed into the machine, one after the other, without snipping the threads between them.

Cross-hatching
A quilting pattern of parallel equidistant lines that run in two directions to form a grid of squares or diamonds.

Directional print
Printed fabric in which there is a distinct direction to the pattern, whether straight or at an angle; for example, stripes, human or animal figures, or some florals.

Ease
To make two pieces of fabric of different sizes fit together in the one seam. One piece may have to be stretched or gathered slightly to bring it to the required length. To ease, first pin the pieces at intervals until they fit, then sew them.

Fat quarter
A piece of fabric that is made by cutting a meter or a yard of fabric in halves first vertically then horizontally. The piece thus cut is approximately 18 x 22 in. (50 x 56 cm).

Feed dogs
The teeth under the sewing plate of a sewing machine, which move to pull the fabric through the machine. The feed dogs must be lowered to allow for free-motion quilting.

Finger pressing
A way of pressing a temporary crease in a piece of fabric, for example when finding the middle of two pieces so that they can be matched before being joined. Running a fingernail along a crease will make it lie flat.

Fussy cut
To cut out a pieced shape centered on a printed motif on the fabric, rather than cutting it out at random.

Grain
The direction of the fabric, along the warp (vertical threads) or the weft (horizontal threads). These are both straight grains, along which woven fabrics do not stretch. Compare with bias.

Half-square triangle
A triangle that is made from a square cut across one diagonal. Half-square triangles have the bias along the hypotenuse (or longest side). Compare with quarter-square triangle.

Mitered corner
A corner that is joined at a 45-degree angle.

Novelty print
A fabric printed with themed designs, such as toys, cartoon characters, or animals.

On point
An arrangement in which the quilt blocks are placed diamond fashion, with their corners at the 12, 3, 6, and 9 o'clock positions, rather than in a square fashion.

Outline quilt
To make one or more outlines of a motif or block design, radiating outward.

Patchwork
A generic term for the process of sewing together many small pieces of fabric to make a quilt; also known as piecework.

Piece
An individual fabric shape that may be joined to other fabric shapes to make a quilt block, or used on its own (in which case it is known as a one-patch). Also known as a patch.
Piecing is the process of joining together pieces of fabric to make a quilt top, a quilt block, or a border.

Pin baste
To pin through the layers of a quilt "sandwich", using safety pins, to hold them together during quilting. The pins are removed once the quilting is complete.

Quarter-square triangle
A triangle that is made from a square, cut across both diagonals. Quarter-square triangles have the bias along the two short sides. Compare with half-square triangle.

Quilt top
The uppermost, decorative layer of a quilt. It may be pieced, appliquéd, or a combination of both, with or without borders.

Quilter's ruler
Precision-cut, straight-edged plastic rulers in various sizes, used with rotary cutters and rotary-cutting (self-healing) mats. They make it easy to cut accurate shapes and to cut through several layers of fabric at once. They come in straight varieties and also those designed for cutting at various angles or for creating triangles.

Quilting
In general, the process of making a quilt; more specifically, the process of stitching patterns by hand or machine through the quilt layers to decorate the quilt, add strength, and anchor the batting inside the quilt.

Quilting frame
A free-standing floor apparatus, made of wood or plastic tubing, in which a quilt is held while it is being quilted.

Quilting hoop
A hand-held circular wooden device in which a quilt is held while being quilted.

Raw edge
The cut edge of a fabric.

Rotary cutter
A cutting device similar in appearance to a pizza cutter, with a razor-sharp circular blade. Used in conjunction with a quilter's ruler and quilting mat, it allows several layers of fabric to be cut at once, easily and with great accuracy.

Rotary-cutting mat
A self-healing plastic mat on which rotary cutters are used. It protects both the blade of the cutter and the work surface beneath the mat during cutting.

Sashing
Strips of fabric that separate blocks in a quilt, to frame them and/or make the quilt larger.

Seam allowance
The margin of fabric between the cut edge and seam line. For quilting and most appliqué, it is ¼ in (6 mm).

Seam line
The guideline that is followed while sewing.

Selvages (selvedges)
The woven finished edges along the length of the fabric.

Setting
The way in which blocks are arranged in a quilt top—for example, square or on point.

Setting square
A plain block or square used with pieced or appliquéd blocks in a quilt top.

Setting triangle
A triangle placed between blocks along the sides of a quilt set on point, to straighten up the edges.

Stash
A quilter's hoard of fabrics.

Template
Plastic, card, or paper shape used for tracing and cutting fabric pieces for piecing or appliqué or to transfer quilting designs to a quilt top.

Walking foot
A special sewing-machine foot that feeds the top layer of a quilt sandwich evenly through the machine, while the feed dogs control the bottom layer.

Warp
The lengthwise threads in a woven fabric, which interlock with the weft threads; see also Weft.

Weft
The widthwise threads in a woven fabric, which interlock with the warp threads; see also warp.

get the skinny

I'm aware that many people who buy my books are just starting out on their quilting journeys, so here are a few bits and pieces, interesting places to go, and sites to shop at.

There are many wonderful bricks-and-mortar quilt shops in the world, and where possible I would encourage you to shop at your local patchwork shop rather than buy online. I'm aware that this isn't always possible, but a local quilt shop will help you select your fabric, give you recommendations and hints, and offer great classes to help you along the way. Your local quilt shop can't survive to hold your classes unless you also shop with them. Viva la Quilt Shop!

Obviously. listing every quilt shop is not possible, so here are a few online shops (that ship worldwide!) I like to visit.

Fabric online

CV Quiltworks
www.cvquiltworks.com

Fabricworm
www.fabricworm.com

Glorious Color
www.gloriouscolor.com

Hawthorne Threads
www.hawthornethreads.com

Pink Chalk Fabrics
www.pinkchalkfabrics.com

Quilt Fabric Delights
www.quiltfabricdelights.com

Sew Mama Sew
www.sewmamasew.com

Notions (haberdashery) online

The question I am asked most when I travel to teach is—what brand do you use? There are thousands of great products out there; these are the brands I prefer at the moment.

For appliqué
Patchwork with Busy Fingers Milliners #11
Aurifil Cotton Mako 50 weight thread
Patchwork with Busy Fingers appliqué glue

For quilting
John James Pebble Crewel Embroidery needles #10
Presencia Finca Perle 8 cotton
Clover open-sided thimble
Bonwick quilting hoop
Matilda's Own 100% cotton batting (wadding)

Perspex ruler sets
Perspex ruler sets are available from me both retail and wholesale for the following quilts in this book:

All That And The Hatter Too
Bangles
Fancy That
I Love All The Colors
Lady Marmalade
Love Beads
Millefiori
Paint By Numbers
String-sane

and also for quilts in several of my previous books. I sell tools for appliqué, fabric packs, scrap bags, and a DVD of my hand appliqué technique.

Visit www.sarah@sarahfielke.com—and yes, I ship worldwide!

Websites for information, online classes, and industry news

Generation Q Magazine
www.generationqmagazine.com

Craftsy
www.craftsy.com

Fat Quarterly
www.fatquarterly.com

iSew Academy
www.isewacademy.com

True Up
www.trueup.net

Whip Up
www.whipup.net

Or join a Quilt Guild near you—you will meet other quilters and be inspired by their work and enriched by their company. I am a member of the Quilters Guild of NSW and the Greater Western Sydney Modern Quilt Guild.

Inspirational blogs for quilts, fabrics, and fun

Quiltville
www.quiltville.blogspot.com

Twin Fibers
www.twinfibers.blogspot.com

Bemused
www.bemused.typepad.com

I'm a Ginger Monkey
www.imagingermonkey.blogspot.com

Mrs Schmenkman Quilts
www.mrsschmenkmanquilts.wordpress.com

Pam Kitty Morning
www.pamkittymorning.blogspot.com

Piece and Press
www.pieceandpress.com

Red Pepper Quilts
www.redpepperquilts.com

The Happy Zombie
www.thehappyzombie.com

For reference

The patterned fabrics used in the Bangles quilt are by Denyse Schmidt for JoAnns Fabrics USA, with thanks to Spotlight Australia.

The solids in the Paint By Numbers quilt are Kona Cottons, with thanks to Robert Kaufman.

Oakshott Fabrics are available from www.oakshottfabrics.com

Dan Sicko's cult-status book which inspired The Bass Line quilt is called Techno Rebels: The Renegades of Electronic Funk.

Find Me Online!

I love answering questions and hearing from those of you who have made my quilts or enjoyed my books. Come and say hi!

Website: www.sarahfielke.com
Blog: www.thelastpiece.net
Email: sarah@sarahfielke.com
Twitter: @sarahfielke
Facebook: /sarah.fielke
Pintrest: sarahfielke
Instagram: sfielke
Flickr: sfielke

Teaching: I teach regular classes in Sydney, and I often teach interstate and overseas.
I teach online classes at Craftsy.com. You can find all the details of my latest classes on my blog, or email me to ask for a class list if you would like me to visit your local shop or group.

index

acknowledgments

My three boys are my whole world. I love you.

Thank you to Cindy for bringing me in to the Cico stable, and to the marketing team at Cico Books for having the faith in me to go forward in a new venture. Your support means everything! Also at Cico, thank you to Penny Craig, Sally Powell and the team behind the scenes, and to my fantastic editor, Sarah Hoggett, and proofreader, Marie Clayton.

Once again, the photography of my wonderful friend Sue Stubbs has made this book so beautiful. Thanks, Sue, for having such a true understanding of me and what I like making!

A HUGE thank you to my super-whizz machine quilter Kim Bradley and her long-suffering husband Dave, who always, always have my back and turn things around in a flash when I'm floundering.

Thank you to Sandy Caller, my stunt binder extraordinaire, who put on so many beautiful bindings for me in my hour of need.

Hugs and love to Belle, Flo, and Rosie, and a special thanks to Amy Lobsiger just for being awesome, and to Anabel Sicko for letting me use her special quilt and its story for the book.

And of course, thanks to all my students and online friends near and far who read my ramblings, tweet me, Facebook me, come to my classes, buy my books, and send me chatty, friendly emails and photos. You are all so amazing and I love each and every one of you for the contributions and laughter you add to my days.